CORRESPONDENCE HALL OF SHAME:

ONE WOMAN'S ADVENTURES IN ONLINE IDIOCY

By Erica Scott

ISBN 9781490407401

TABLE OF CONTENTS

For those who are classy, thoughtful, and kind (and at least semi-literate!). Thank you for existing!

And, as always, for John.

WHAT IS THE "CORRESPONDENCE HALL OF SHAME"?

Those who know me and have been following my blogs for years are quite familiar with this periodic feature of my blog (*Erica Scott: Life, Love and Spanking*). But for those who aren't, allow me to enlighten and (hopefully) entertain.

Years ago when I entered the Internet world, I quickly discovered what a double-edged sword it was. The plusses were many, including having the world at my fingertips: I could communicate with people I'd never have encountered otherwise. Strangers reached out to me and became my friends. As I got into the kink scene and became what's known as a "spanking model" (performing in videos), I gained an online following via several forums and then my blog, which I started in 2005. I got a lot of lovely compliments and kind words of appreciation. But on the flip side, there were unwelcome encounters. Rude, presumptuous, badly written and/or obscene Instant Messages, comments, emails, and replies to my various spanking ads. While I have had the same boyfriend since 1996 and am happily in love, I do engage in spanking play with other men and have always had ads open. Out of respect for my relationship, I am very specific about seeking spanking only, not sex. But despite any amount of clarity, that and other parts of my profiles are often ignored (including the oh-so-important "I do not switch").

My reaction to these messages was anger and frustration. Where did people get off, writing such drivel to me? Granted, I understand that putting oneself out on the Internet, particularly in the kink world, carries some risks, and one must take the bad with the good. But some of this stuff was ridiculous. You can get down and dirty once you know someone, if they like that sort of thing. However, introducing yourself that way is generally not the best idea. Also, if you're writing to someone for the very first time, wouldn't it seem practical to make some sort of attempt at a good first impression, and not send a lot of X-rated text-speak? And to take a moment to actually *read* about what they're seeking?

I didn't want to reply to any of this, as I didn't wish to engage. Still, I found myself fantasizing about telling them exactly what I thought. Then it dawned on me: Why not? No, not actually reply to any of the wankers. But what if I started a blog feature, in which I would copy and paste these God-awful correspondences (eliminating all identifiers), and then would add what I *wished* I could answer back? Not only would this give me some satisfaction, but it might amuse my readers as well. Hence, the Correspondence Hall of Shame (CHoS) column was born in 2007.

Since then, I've had many outrageous entries and the CHoS is well known in the spankers' blogosphere. Many have said over the years that I should write a book with all this material I've gathered. I believe I've got enough of these tidbits now to do just that.

What you will see in the following chapters is the (almost) verbatim messages I received. I have edited out any names, phone numbers, and email addresses. But the remainder is untouched, so every typo, misspelling, grammatical gaffe, and obscenity is intact. Following each message is my pithy rejoinder. (Some of the entries go back a few years, so you'll notice I'm several different ages, and a few references are dated.) Just to be clear, with a couple of noted exceptions, I never actually sent any of these answers; they're simply what I would have liked to say. And yes, there is plenty of sarcasm.

What this book is *not*: A forum for ridicule of those for whom English is a second language, or those with learning disabilities, lack of education, etc. While I weep for the sorry state of literacy in this country, I'm not writing this to make fun of people. I have gotten many notes and messages over the years from people who do not write/spell well, but they are polite, respectful, and nice. I absolutely *do not* include these in the CHoS; I am just as kind in return as they were to me. But if my correspondents write badly *and* they are rude, nasty, overly familiar, etc., then anything is fair game. Contrary to what my detractors may believe, I am not mean just for meanness' sake. But push me first, and I push back, in my signature snarky fashion.

Also, I've had many friends jokingly say, "I hope I never end up in the CHoS!" or "Uh-oh, is that typo I made going into the CHoS?" Rest assured: I never included anything my friends have written in the Correspondence Hall of Shame. It is not a vehicle I use to ridicule people I care about. I may tease some friends (particularly tops) about their typos, but only the nameless, faceless strangers get the dubious honor of being featured in the CHoS.

For my female friends: You know you've gotten messages like these! This book is sweet (imagined) revenge for us all! And for my male friends: Some of you may cringe reading this, feeling that your gender has been irreversibly besmirched by these idiots. Just the opposite, actually. I appreciate you good guys even more, now!

I promise you that I have not made any of these correspondences up. I'd swear to God or on a stack of bibles or something like that, but coming from an atheist, I guess that would be pretty worthless. But I give you my solemn word.

Finally, for those who don't know me, I am a proofreader/copyeditor by trade. So yes, I do have a deep appreciation for good grammar and spelling. However, for the record, I hate, loathe, and despise the term "Grammar Nazi." The Nazis were heartless, murderous, anti-Semitic thugs, who beat and tortured people and threw them in ovens. Likening a person who insists upon proper grammar to a Nazi is not only insulting, but frankly, it's fucking ignorant.

If you must employ some sort of title, then I'm all right with "Grammar Police," or something along that line. You can even say I'm a bit anal about good grammar, and I won't argue with you. But that Nazi bit needs to be retired. Permanently.

All right, off the soapbox, and on with the hilarity. Enjoy!

THE QUICK AND THE DENSE

Some of these messages, as you will see later, are quite lengthy and detailed. But many others are quickies, and in their way, even more outrageous than the longer ones, because they cram the maximum of stupidity into the minimum of verbiage. Honestly, is it that difficult to fully and correctly spell out a few words? Is their Shift key wired to give them an electric shock? I thought I'd feature some of those first; a sort of appetizer, if you will. Here's the format, which applies to the rest of the book: The indented copy blocks in the sans serif font are the original messages, and the comments following are what I replied in the CHoS.

According to Shakespeare, brevity is the soul of wit. Not with these beauties!

    i hope u got a msn or aim..cuz i m hot

I m sorry u r so hot. Maybe u should take a cold shower.

    can i give you an huge cock will that work baby

I really couldn't tell you whether or not yours works, and frankly, I'd rather not find out, but thank you.

    hey sexy wanna see some cock??

Well, now that you mention it, why yes, I would! Good thing I'm going over to John's house later tonight, huh? Thanks for reminding me—have a nice day!

YOU AER SEXY BABBY

Babby???

do you want spank my ass!!! yes or no? im your servant!!lol

Um, no. I'm a bottom. I get spanked. I don't spank. Nowhere in my profile or in my blog or anywhere else does it imply that I want to spank anyone. You want to be my servant? OK, fine—here's your first order. Go write 100 times: "I will read profiles thoroughly before I write stupid messages."

how r u lady
dam you so hot

Yeah, me so hot. Me live in San Fernando Valley and it be effing hot, mon. Dam? Is there some sort of beaver joke in there somewhere?

Be prepared to get your ass tow up.

Huh?? Tow up? Is AAA going to be involved in this? I suppose he meant "tore up" (and that's just so lovely, isn't it?). Yup, nothing makes my little heart go pitty-pat like a man telling me he's going to tear up my ass.

come here let me make that pretty ass cherry red baby

I ain't your baby, sweet pea. And I don't have that much experience with farm animals, but I've never seen a cherry-red ass. Perhaps with a few buckets of food coloring, it could be achieved. But really, one should have better things to do.

> do you want a spanking from me littlegirl?

I dunno; who are you? Don't misunderstand me—if I got this message from someone I know, and like, and want to play with, it could be a hot little surprise in the middle of my day. But I don't know this person from a hole in the wall. All I know is that he doesn't appear to have a Shift key on his keyboard, that he doesn't know how to use a comma, and he is unaware that "little girl" is two words.

> id love to give you a good spanking after you gave me a footjob ;)

Someone needs to enlighten me here. I know what a handjob is…what the hell is a footjob? Does that entail my doing something to his feet? Or is it like a handjob, only using my feet instead? (and how clumsy would *that* be?)

> i wud like 2 psnak u but i might wanna be naked while i do that 2 u

Excuse me? You wud like to *what* me?? And as for that naked business—sorry, honey. I have been across many laps, and hope to be across many more, but there is only one man who gets to psnak me while he's naked.

can yo explain what is the you are looking for

Yo, Rocky. What is the you no understand? I was is clear perfectly.

u are very sexy feets...i wanna see u feets...i have the webcam..

And I have the delete button. (click)

wow... love you'R pics.
Wish i could see you naked

You know, I didn't think there were any more ways to screw up your/you're, but you did it, honey. You wish you could see me naked? Yeah, I'm sure you do. I wish I could win the lottery. That's not going to happen either.

I'd fuck you like you've never been fucked before.

Oh, really—and how would that be...badly?

with an ass like your after i spank it i would and must kiss it

With an ass like my what? And yes, buddy, you can certainly kiss my ass.

ur fine ill have sex with u 4 3 fuckin hours

Geeez, at least he could take me to dinner first. But then again, I'd have to drive, and I'd probably have to pay for it, too. Because he's 15. Fifteen?? What the hell is a 15-year-old doing, propositioning a 50-year-old? I know some guys like older women, but come on. I could be his grandmother, for God's sake.

Anyway, he also sent me a friend request, which I denied. A few minutes later, I got this:

ey be my frind so we can talk about sex

Yeah, right. Tell you what, folks—do me a favor. If the day comes that I am so desperate and pathetic that I have to resort to talking about sex with an illiterate 15-year-old, just shoot me in the head, OK?

can u plz add me i have a hard 11inch cock waiting 4 u

Sure you do, honey. And I have a nice pair of 38 DDs where you can nestle that puppy. By the way…this writer was also 15. WTF?

im sitting here bored and dreaming of spankings can i call you ?

Dream on.

id like to spank your ass with this dick

(looking at the photo he so generously supplied) Thanks, but I don't think I'd feel that.

great pics....love your as.......

Oh, for heaven's sake. Now they're too lazy to even type the second s?

13

Another one with a sluggish "s" finger:

Nice profile pic. Is that your freshly spanked as?

As what? Nah, that's not me. Some strange woman just happened to appear bare-assed in my bedroom.

damn id let you suck my dick any day baby

I didn't ask you if I could. But thank you for the offer.

i like your pictures i wish i caan spanke that

No, I'm sorry, you caan't. And what the hell is *spanke*? Is that the way they spelled it in olden days? Did they have the equivalent of today's adult toy stores in Victorian times, called Ye Olde Spanke Shoppe?

gosh I love your redish ASS!
sorry if that was too open I just cant controll my emotions

You can't spell, either. Are you trying to say that my bottom is reddish, or that it resembles a radish? And if you can't controll [sic] your emotions, I don't want to think about what else you can't controll, either.

talk about your prefect little ass ..damn lady
love have you over my knee

Well, there's a new one. I looked up "prefect" on Dictionary.com, and here is the first definition listed:

"A person appointed to any of various positions of command, authority, or superintendence, as a chief magistrate in ancient Rome or the chief administrative official of a department of France or Italy."

You read it here, folks—my little ass commands authority. I don't know what that means, but it sounds good.

someone told me that u been very bad & that u need a Spanking

(jaw dropping) Wow, ya think?

wats up sexy
wat u doin

Wat I doin? Deleting ur message.

You fucking dirty old bitch....

Excuse me? OLD? Now that hurt.

And get this...know what this guy's screen name is? Romeo! Romeo, o Romeo, wherefore art thy head? Up thy posterior?

what do you like to do thats kinky ?i like kinky to

You like kinky to what? Here's an idea—try actually reading my profile first, before you ask questions that have already been clearly answered. I think it's quite obvious what I'm into.

nice ass baby hit me back.

OK, I'd be glad to hit you back. Would you prefer a slap upside the head or a punch in the nose?

damn u r a hottie u into blk dick at all sexy?

Once you go blk, you never go bck.

cal I spank u?

No, u cal not.

Hey so what do i have to do to get yuor number

Well, let's see...
1. An introduction would be nice.
2. You're only 19, so you could age several years rapidly.
3. Learn how to spell "your." It's a simple little word.

like i wish i was there and you was with me .the things ill do to you

Like, I'm glad you isn't here. I'm already ill just reading this.

luv the flexible pic purple panties r sexy i wish i had them

You wish you had my panties? I'm afraid to ask why. To wear? To sleep with? To...never mind. I don't want to know.

a u like to be a bad girl

a yeah i do. how'd u guess?

> damn sexxy.. man do i wanna fuck and eat yo
> pussy mami

I ain't yo mami, chump. If I were, I'd wash yo mouth out with soap.

> I don't mind doing you in public as long as you
> are comfotible with it.

I'm sorry; I must have missed something here. I don't remember saying I'd like you to do me in public. Oh, wait...I didn't. And guess what? I don't want you to do me in private, either.

> u wanna c what your pics r doin to me? wanna
> c on my cam?

Uh, that would be no, and no.

> my god woman what a delectable eddable ass
> you have...makes my tongue hard!!!!!

Oh, good. Because there's nothing worse than a flaccid tongue.
Eddable??

> i luv your hott and sexxy picturtes

Can someone explain the practice of adding extra letters to words? Is that for some sort of emphasis, or what? Hott? Sexxy? Oh, and I had no idea there were two t's in "pictures."

wow sexy love to cum

I'm sure you do, dear. Tell me, have you ever actually done so with a living, breathing, real woman, or is your right hand the love of your life?

sorry for being so direct but I wanna spank you hours and hours and fuck after it..

Interesting thought process: "Maybe if I apologize in advance, I can be as crass as I want and it'll be OK." Think again, moron.

Nice butt. To bad your not into the old in and out.

This is news to me! Since when? And all these years I thought I was enjoying sex. Who was that moaning, writhing woman—my slutty twin?

are you sure you don't want to trade pix with my girlfriend and i?

I'm quite positive. And it's "my girlfriend and me." My girlfriend and ME, dammit. Why can't people grasp the simple concept of subjective vs. objective pronouns? It's enough to make I scream.

cute is cute and your a fuckin damn cuite!

You heard it here, people. I'm not just cute—I'm fuckin damn cute. (I'm going to assume that *cuite* was meant to be "cutie.")

u like that dick to be slapped against that ass huh

No, not particularly. That's kind of thuddy, and I prefer sting over thud. Or, most likely in your case, it would feel kind of wet noodle-y.

can i ask you a question since ur a girl?????????

I'm a girl? Thank you for noticing! But no, with an intro like that, I don't think I want to know what your question is.

hey bb. i wana spank u nd i want u to spank me back.

I don't spank, brainiac. And who the hell is bb??

nice pix what i have to do to get in that ass

Hmmm, let me think…Maybe learn how to communicate properly? Don't say things like "get in that ass"?

wow can i spank u then lick ur ass

I really don't know how I'm going to turn down such a lovely offer, but I'm going to force myself.

dang ur pretty thin for a woman ur age u don t like to eat?

What kind of body is a "woman my age" supposed to have? Morbidly obese? Breasts in my lap and butt slapping the back of my knees? And yes, I love to eat. Doesn't mean I do so every waking minute.

By the way, I checked out this guy's profile—his picture was of his naked stomach and chest. He's half my age, and his belly had more rolls than a bakery. Sour grapes, perhaps?

I'd love to spank & fuck your ass.

(gasp) Bestiality! It's bad enough that these pervs want to spank poor innocent farm animals, but now they want to have sex with them too? Oh, the humanity.

paddle mashing into two hills soft ass meat, give's me a woody!

Oh, this is so wrong, on so many levels. Soft ass meat?? Who are you calling soft, pal? I'll bet my butt is harder than you'll ever be. And another pet peeve—why do people insist on adding apostrophes where they don't belong? "Give's" would be a contraction of "give is," which makes no sense. Moron.

Spanker Seeks Ass

Why don't you just look in the mirror?

r u a milf?

No, I never had kids. Too afraid they might turn out like you.

> Good you please send me some pics and bids.
> I'm sooo horny.

This one took me a minute, but I finally figured it out. He meant to say, "Could you send me some pics and vids?" Well, that makes more sense. The answer is still no, however.

> cant wait to spank ur ass and make u cream

Can't wait? Well then, by all means, let's set up a time. How about never? Is never good for you?

> Hi,, nice spankable ass,, wowowo

Feeeeelllliiiiings, wowowo, feeeeelllliiiiiings…And what's up with the double commas?

> do u like being called mommy?

Well, let's see. For one thing, I'm not a top. For another, I underwent rather uncomfortable surgery to ensure I'd never be a mother. Does that answer your question? No? How about this, then…Hell, NO!

From a 19-year-old:

> i love ur long legs and booty babe ;]

Ah, thanks, babe. And I love that sweet li'l soft spot on the crown of your head.

> I am a do who is interisted in spanking. Nothig
> else.

I believe it. Clearly you're not interisted [sic] in spelling properly. You're not a do, you're a don't.

This is from a 22-year-old. I am exactly 2 1/2 times his age; scary. I don't get it! When I was 22, an "older man" was 30.

hey maybe u can show me a thing or two?

Maybe I can. Here are a couple of things. 1. the correct way to spell "u" is y-o-u; 2. here's one of my favorite sweatshirts. It's got "Beatlefest '81" printed on it. Which means I have clothing older than you.

r u still in bed well ask me in

I'm not in bed, but you must be, because you're dreaming.

so u liked to be spank what do u have guys spank u with?

I like to have guys spank me with finesse and intelligence, toots.

u r fuckin sexy

Concise; I like that. And hey, he completely spelled out one word out of four.

I would luv 2 spank u bebe

I don't know who this Bebe is, but perhaps she likes online shorthand better than I do.

well as long as I have a face u have a place too sit !!!!

Not going *too* happen, douchebag. I'd rather sit on an anthill.

i realy love you ass.

Thank you. I realy [sic] *don't* love you, ass.

i have a raging hard on right now! what should i do?

Don't look at *me*!

ur sexy i would eat ur pussy all night long

Honey, if that's all you want to do all night, you're either suffering from lack of imagination, or you're overcompensating for certain deficiencies elsewhere, methinks.

hey erica your gorgous id luv ot spank you

"id luv ot"…You know, sometimes these people boggle my mind. How do they function in life if they misspell three out of three simple words?

Well If your Avalible for day time spankings let me know a we'll talk about it…

Um…no, we won't.

your smokin hot an nice feet an everything else you have. merry chriastmas babe

Oh, for *chriast's* sake. Sorry, babe, wrong fetish.

crazy bitch ;-)

Well now, I resent that. I am not crazy. My mother had me tested. Mildly neurotic, yes. But not crazy.

I wonder what your ass tastes like...

I'm guessing it's ass-flavored. But you'll never find out.

Lady u look good to eat

I might need some tenderizing first. I'm a tough old bird.

i bet your a hoot in bed like a little gumby doll

Hmmm...if I'm Gumby, I guess that makes you Pokey? (dating myself with that reference) Eat your heart out, pumpkin. Only one man knows what a hoot I am in bed, and it isn't you.

wow u show alot of skin

Yes, I do. What's your point?

hi, you have a dynomite smile and a cute hieny

DynoMITE! Thank you, J.J. What's a hieny? Is that anything like a hyena? Mine is laughing at the moment.

like to hammer that body, hook up?

Hammer, hook...do I look like a nail to you? Go hammer yourself on the head. I'll let you choose which one.

> i want to give life to the bed with you mama,can i ?....

I'm sorry to break this to you, dear, but beds are inanimate objects. You can't give life to them. And I ain't your mama.

> ok, ur HOT n u know ur HOT, n i would spank n do u all day long, pretty feet

All right, it's bad enough that "ur" means you're and "u" means you. But since when did "n" become text-speak for *and*?

> Add me n0w n cum t0 me n get ur spankings

Again with the n. And this one can't tell a zero from an o. We are truly going to hell in a hand basket, people.

> hey sexy! watz good?

Not your spelling of *what's*, that's for sure.

> I have a taste in my mouth could it be you mmmm

That one left me absolutely speechless. If you guys have a clever rejoinder, please, do share.

let me get you'r number so we can talk damn
you'r sexy as fuck

Sure, here ya go—1-800-438-5678. (pssst—that spells
out 1-800-GET-LOST.)

can i set up an oppoinment, to give u a
spankin...lol

Honey, if you can't even spell "appointment," then
no, you can't have one.

U want a big 18 year cock?

Tsk...does your mama know you're messing around
with the computer again? Go back to your playpen
before she sees that you're missing.

you into family sex?

Please. Have you *seen* my family??

hi babe....you look gorceous...do u trade

Hey, I'm gorceous! (what's gorceous?) Trade what?
Never mind, don't answer that.

Baby you are hot in frozen in ice yummy

Again, speechless. I leave this one to you, folks.

Im lookin for afew new pets who kno their
place

Uh huh. Good luck with that. I'm looking for a few articulate men. *Kno* any?

u r soo hot baby

(yawn) OK, if u say so. Big points for originality, dude.

whats up? u like younger cock?

What's up? Apparently, you are. Well, it really depends on the younger man who is attached to the younger cock. In your case, I'm thinking probably not.

a profissional spanker is waiting to chat with you

Keep waiting. And if you're going to claim to be one, it might be helpful to learn how to spell *professional*.

i am very orel

Orel?? As in Hershiser? There's no spanking in baseball!

i want to spank u with my hard thick cock

Considering the damage I've done to some hard thick hands, I don't think you want to risk that, sugar.

i love too spank you on your bare ass

Around the likes of you, my ass stays clothed, thank you.

> hi im xxxx love to call u see how things go u look so youg and so sensual

Youg? Do you have a cold?

> how you like to be spank otk or what bye hand ????

I like be spank bye men who write good.

> im tall sexy and a big cock

Yes, I'm sure you're a big cock. Whether or not you *have* one is yet and forever to be seen.

> yes baby oil all over u.......slipping and sliding all over u//////then what next

Then u slip and slide right out the door, and don't let it hit you in the slash.

> you do prefer white meat correct?

That depends. I don't care for pork. But I do like chicken breasts. They're so much lower in fat and when prepared properly, they are as juicy and flavorful as thighs or drumsticks.

I trust this answers your question?

> hey sex you have a nice ass i would spank you all nite

Whatever. Mind if I sleep while you're doing that?

I could totally eat that ass!

Don't be ridiculous. What would I sit on if you did that?

id luv 2 meat u sexy ;o)

I'll just bet you'd luv 2 *meat* me, honey. So, was that an intentional play on words, or is he simply too illiterate to know how to spell *meet*?

hi sexy how r u i would love to give u a bad ass spanking

You think I have a bad ass? Gee, some people like it.

The next three share a common theme:

Can you like animal sex ???

I don't know, can I? If you're talking about fucking like bunnies, then yes. If you're talking about actually fucking the bunnies, then go away.

Are you into animal sex also ?

Does the occasional and regrettable encounter with swine count?

I very like your pix. are u into K9 sex also, beside BDSM ??

I've been with a few dogs in my time, but I draw the line at the four-legged variety.

i too luv 2 spank on my buttoks

You know, it's a lot more fun when someone *else* spanks on your buttoks.

can u handle powerful MASTER?

Yup—I click DELETE.

I'm still amazed buy the shape of your but

My but what?

love how you're bottom swells after a good spanking.

Does it? This is news to me. Perhaps I should give my top a tape measure for a before-and-after. Or maybe I've been eating too many peanut butter Oreos.

Master would like to be friends

Sorry. Erica would not.

r u willing to meet,obey,serve......lets get together

r u willing to bother reading my profile, u stupid ass?

wanna spank me ? call xxx xxx-xxxx only if UR a woman or shemail

Shemail? Is that, like, email from a woman?

I deleted the above, and next day, I heard from him again:

> thats ok if i coud at least spank u & U me that wood be nice

I don't care how nice your wood is. I'm not going to spank u.

> Little lady u r beyond all thats real,no way to explain u.

"Little lady"? Who are you, John Wayne's ghost? And really, what's to explain? I may be a complex woman, but I'm not quantum physics.

> Do u butter those buns?

No, that's not healthy. I use Smart Balance margarine.

> I would love to soank you till it hurts

Is this meant to be a threat? It's *supposed* to hurt, fleabrain. Oh, and before you do it, learn how to spell it.

Are you warmed up now? Has your brain started to melt yet? You ain't seen nothing yet; we're just getting started! At this point, I'd like to suggest that you put away any beverages; drinking while reading the rest of this book may result in spit-takes.

THE GREAT GASBAG

With all apologies to F. Scott Fitzgerald, of course.

You know this type of correspondent when you see him (or her, but for the sake of simplicity, I'm going to stick with the male pronoun)—the Form Letter writer. This person is not writing to you as an individual; he is casting his long-winded nonsense out into the waters and hoping his dream girl will come floating to him in a bottle, buoyed by his magical words. However, having seen several of these missives, I really cannot imagine how anyone could consider replying to any of them.

I am Master S/M and Dom.ten yeares.
My lady,you very,very nice.Your fhotos very,very goods.
I love woman´s Submissives and Slaves nices.I love woman´s nices.I love Sex anal and oral.
I have one fetiche,foots woman´s nices,your foots my lady very,very nices.Bigs kisses.
In Portugal i have one Slave Bi.Sorry,i not fhotos my Slave whit woman´s.
My lady nice,visit our Profile.We have 14 fhotos Bondage my Slave and two woman´s Submissives Lisbon.We have sessions Bondage and Sex 3,4 sometimes month.
My lady nice,if you accep our invitation,we have two Albuns fhotos,one 15 fhotos my Slave and me Sex,three fhotos my piss and fhotos my Slave Bondage.One Albun 12 fhotos Bondage

my Slave,one fhoto is my Slave kiss the mouth one woman Submissive Bi.

My lady nice,i am and my Slave persons much honests and goods friends.We love friends my lady nice.

My family and my Slave is Ca.My family is San Francisco (Hayward),my Slave is San Rafael,alive and me in Portugal two yeares.

My lady nice,i love your Country.I love Ca.my lady nice.I holidays in Ca.yeares 1998,2004 and 2007 in the month the March 10 days the days 12 to 21 in Hayward.Very,very goods.I love Ca.my lady nice.I love your Country,is my 2 Country.We have goods friends in Ca.my lady nice.In Encino we not friends.

I am Judge in Airoport Lisbon,Custons Cheff 7 persons.

My Slave is Secretary in Embassy U.S.A. Lisbon.

My lady nice,three fhotos Bondage my Slave for you ok?

My Slave legacy one kiss for you much respect.

Big kiss my lady nice,nice:

MASTER S/M.

I swear, I did not alter a word of this. Is your head exploding right about now? Join the club. Read on.

Hi pretty,

.......I am [name deleted].I'm a cute good looking guy... I have Blue eyes, black hair and 5.9ft.I am into building construction.I am a building contractor.I like making new friends because its fun at times knowing someone new and special. I'm seeking for a woman with a beautiful heart, who loves intimacy and caring, a woman who's ready to give as much Love i will give to her. I really was marvelled reading your profile and i enjoyed doing so.. The first thing that came to my mind when i saw your picture was."WOW" you're drop dead GORGEOUS.lol.. I do not want Mrs perfect what i actually want is mrs right so she can be my other half.she will be the neck while i am the head....so i thought it will be nice to let you know that someone out here care's to know more about you, and what I care about is you are Beautiful and I wish to be the man you've always wanted and i'm sure you and I would work things nicely being together. My personality traits are Simple, I'm very Sincere and Honest when it comes to sharing Feelings and Emotions with that speical woman. Perfect, what i actually want is Mrs. Right, so she can be my better half, so she can be neck while am the head. I Love to hold hands while walking on the streets, I love to hug and to spoil as well. I am very passionate, emotional and affectionate person.Right now, i live by myself with my daughter and searching for my soul mate, someone i will spend my eternity with..My favorite color is blue,my hopes and dreams in life is to find my soul mate someday, that's why i decided to try the online dating, though am new to this and want to see how things go on here. I've been single for a while now trying to find myself a real love. I like playing basketball,volleyball and soccer. As I came across your profile you seem to posses some sought of magnetic charm that elicited my interest and fascination. My admiration and physical attraction drew forth my immediate response without hesitation because you appeal to my dreams, desire and taste. My sudden instinctive response was based primarily on a spontaneous mutual attraction which rendered me helpless and unable to resist communicating with you immediately, Please afford me the opportunity to know you. I would like to be the love you are looking and you be the one that I am looking for.Distance is not a barrier as long as our hearts connect as one. Distance between two hearts is not an obstacle; rather a great reminder of just how strong true love can be,Distance does not matter if two hearts are loyal to one another.Your beauty and sweetness captured my heart,I believe a lot can be sensed about a person just from their eyes and their smile! Only God's creations can compare to the beauty that I see in you, The greatest gift to my eyesight is having my eyes set on you. They say,' A picture is worth a thousand words,' but when I saw yours, I was speechless.I was in a cathedral when I got down on my knees and worshipped you, mistook you for an angel without those two celestial wings.looking forward in hearing back from you. My yahoo id is add me i'm online now (xxxxxxxxxxxxxx)I wait to receive your letters soon.

Isn't that *speical*? Where does one start with this pile of cheese? Go ahead, read it a few times, so you will fully appreciate it.

Just call me Goddess Erica, Angel without Wings. (Do I need to go save someone from suicide so I can earn my wings? Where's George Bailey when I need him?)

I'm the neck and he's the head?? How romantic. So he's a disembodied head floating around, looking for a neck to attach to? Yes, we'd be the Frankenstein couple.

He was speechless? Could have fooled me!

I know that this mail will come to you as a surprise, as i came across ur profile as i was browsing through the profiles here and i became so much interested in it that i could not resist it and i have to drop you this few lines to tell you know that i xxxxx is very much interested in you here. I have learnt to be strong and to go for what i see and as i like your profile i hope you don't mind us getting to know each other for a relationship. My name is xxxxx and i am 35yrs old single man living in xxxxxxxxx. I am 1.75cm tall chocolate in complexion with black hair and brown eyes. I am a man with much understanding and love who also appreciates understanding honesty love care and truth. I believe in co-operate exsistence in my relationship which i believe is the best for a matured relationship. I will be very happy if you would find my interest in you to be a thing of happiness and drop me few lines of reply so that we can start from there. I really want to know you better if you don't mind because i always believe love to be the power that can bring two together from afar or near and i hope you will get hold of this point as i do too.I am waiting to hear from you soon and please don't keep me waiting in vain and pains for your reply. You can reply me directly at my e-mail address [deleted] so that i can send you my photos and tell you more about myself.

Good afternoon. i really don't want to know more about yourself, sorry for your pains. Your interest in me is a thing of annoyance and i wish your exsistence would stop exsisting. Please directly go away.

hello dear ,

am xxxx by name 53years old from xxxx

how are you doing toady hope all is well with you well am so delighted that you took your time to write back that i must say you are really decent in attitudes you know,well am an englisn man well i am an international aid worker dear,i am involve in helpinmg less priviledge ones and orphans thats why i dont have time for women out in the street and after the death of my wife dear thats why i have to come online to search for a soul mate and some i would be together with for enternity and i would love us tom start from some where like knowing who we are better dear,whatb do you think well dear here is my mail adress again,please do leave yours or you can add me dear,here is my addy [deleted] ,well i am looking forward in expecting yours,

Where to start, where to start. I've never written to this man before in my life, so he clearly has me confused with someone else. He wants someone he can be with for eternity? Sorry, but unless you're a vampire, that's not possible. Very noble that he helps orphans—I just hope he doesn't help them with their schooling.

Hello,

I do hope these thoughts find you in the best of care and add a smile to your face.

Truly this in all new to me responding to an ad with an introductory email, however the simplicity of what you wrote in you ad got my attention. I admire your directiness. I must give you a compliment..

I am looking to meet one Woman of Substance to spend some quality time with in an attempt to get acquainted.

I am a Single Black Man 54 interested in getting to know you...I do not know if you are open minded in away that you are open to the new adventure of interacial dating. If you would allow yourself to be open in this way I do believe I will add a gentle touch to your life and create an entire new world of happiness with you. You can be the center of attention in my world...I do know how to treat a Lady.....

I am 5'11", 210 lbs., in great physically, mental, financial, spiritual, and emotional condition. I am single and a no non sense type of Man..... I enjoy the simple things in life. movies, music, dancing, cooking, wine tasting, playing chess.. I am romantic, and enjoy kissing and cuddling, and I am looking for a Monogamous relationship long term. I do realize it takes time to get to know someone and I am a patient Man..... I am a Christian Man an I do believe in God and have morals and standards an I value family... I am open minded and looking for only one special woman to share the desires of my heart with everyday.

If you are interested I am available...I am for real and do not play games. YOU have my attention.

I am available to IM or talk on the telephone. Communication is most important. Tell me more about yourself. What is your name? When is your birthday? How would you like to be my special Valentines?

I look forward to hearing from you.
Have a wondeful day.

I'm so sorry, dear Man, but I'm going to have to decline, as we are a complete mismatch. No, not because I'm white and you're black, but because I'm a reasonably intelligent individual and you're an idiot. What's my name?? You write me all this twaddle and you didn't even notice what my name is? Oh, and my birthday is on the same day that you'll meet me—the 22nd of Never.

> Hi, I'm [deleted].I live and work in California.I'm An Hair Stylist By profession.I have a good Sense of humour.I'm White/caucasian..I have been divorced for the past 5yrs..i am Highly interested in geting to know more about you.My ID at yahoo is [deleted].so i will like you to get back to me with your yahoo messenger Id if u do have so that we can be able to chat over there and get to know each other very well.So I'll like you to kindly get back to me with your Id so that we can be able to get connected.I am A God Fearing man who goes to church regularly.i do not smoke neither drink no take drugs.I Recite Poems and poetry for fun when i am less busy.I'm a new member here...I'm online now on yahoo messenger. Hope to Read from you Soonest. Stay Bless in Christ.

Do women actually answer these? I wish I knew if they were for real. I mean, every one of them seems to share the same characteristics: 1) they're all illiterate; 2) they're all hyper-religious; and 3) they're all on Yahoo messenger. Sometimes I think as an experiment, I should contact one of them, but then I think again, and...nahh!

hi there ...my name is xxxxx and i think i really like what i read abt you .i would want to be your friend at least from there we can step forward in whatever faith has for us.This is the time for me to step out of the shadows of my life and share the spotlight with my leading woman. I am free to move beyond the stage where I have watched life's drama unfold before my eyes.I want to fulfill a role that I have before me.I do not pretend to be something I am not. I have played many roles in my life.All the roles and bit parts where the stepping stones to my future. I am discovering who I am and what I truly am about.My time has come to quit waiting in the wings and take my place in this world.

Share the spotlight? Leading woman? Move beyond the stage? Life's drama? Roles and bit parts? Waiting in the wings? Tell me, are there any actor's clichés this guy missed?

have 30 + years of experience, am skilled in almost all facets of the lifestyle, enjoy breast bondage, nipple play, oral, anal, and a good woman who is dedicated and serves me because she wants to. I have a 3bdrm home, a 1200 sq ft workshop I am remodeling into a dungeon, and I seek a good woman to join me here and enhance this home of mine. age means nothing to me, the more novice the better as there are less bad habits to break.Maturity and knowledge count for something, experience and wisdom also. I am strict, firm, but careing and thoughtful. I provide all necessities for my partner, including a good social life, a stable home, good training, protection mentally and physically, and require no outside work.I would think that in this uncertain day and age that there would be a good real slave ready to accept a good home. If your tired of the chase, the pain of the fakes and frauds, tired of the search and not finding what you seek, drop me a line ok.I am a totally open Master, I do beleave this is a two way street, and that a real true sub/slave will overlook the small things in life, as we are all not perfect. My messenger is xxxxxxxxxx at y Hope to talk to you there.I will make the first contact, the rest is up to you if your willing to take it further your contact to me is necessary, I will not chase, I have the means and ways of making a good life, and I am certain one who seeks it will find me.

He's not going to chase me?? Boohooooo! I'm crushed!

Please tell me that no one would seriously respond to this. Please, please, please. I'm begging here. I'll bet his stable home is literally a stable.

Hello

I am doing great well here and i hope and pray that every thing should be well there with you and the family over there.Any way i may say you will be surprise to see this my mail but i want to tell you that you shouldn't be surprise for this mail because i was viewing through members here and i came across you profile which made me very interesting encourage me more to get to know you better and if you don't mind i will be in good position to request for friendship between us and i hope this my mail will meet your kindest conviction and i will be taken by you as my friend,by the my name is Xxxxxxx and i will be very grateful if you could take me as your friend here so that we can share and also learn from each other and even more,i will like to know more about you and i will tell you more when i get a respond from you very soon.I thank God for giving me this wonderful opportunity to come across this precious profile of yours and i will what am writing for will be taking in consideration and serious as well.Bye for now and hope to read from you very soon.

Your Newly Friend

Just a suggestion—when you can't write well, don't try to make up for that by writing more. It doesn't work. That precious profile of mine?? My head...

This next one isn't the typical form letter, but it definitely fits in the long-winded category. A bit of background: This man was on FetLife, had all of two friends, and was very clearly enamored with himself.

I fly my own aircraft, have travelled in 51 couitries, been on Expeditions and even had the National Geographic Society exhibited 3 of my films on their Adventure Series. But of all these facets, the one thing that I've always cherrish the most was in finding a real Lady. There are many, many ladies around these day but I want to meet a Lady with a high degree of self esteem ... and you sound like that person. When I interviewed Hugh Hufner for a TV short, I realized his key to success with ladies was that he always was a perfect gentleman.

Here's a tip, darlin'. Name-dropping doesn't impress me. But if you're going to do it anyway, at least make damn sure you spell the name correctly! Hufner, indeed.

Apparently, the above gentleman saw his mention in the CHoS. I then received this (not so) little gem:

Hi Erica: You wrote an article in your column recently in which you criticized me for using Hugh Hefner's name. You said that I was NAME DROPING because I couldn't spell Hefner correctly.

Before I used it, I check it again to see if it was spelled Heffner or Hefner? The last was correct. The error that occurred was simply a TYPO error and nothing more. I asked [my friend] to forward my reply to you where ever you were which she may or may not have done. So as a fellow published author, I though that I would pass along this informaton so that you could print a retraction!

[My friend] was sure that I was name dropping and chided me for it. So I asked her this question?

"Where in the sporting world do you find the name Hugh Hefner?"

She hadn't the feintest idea and neither did any of her friends. Some came up with stupid, dumb assed answers which they thought were funny. They weren't. The answer lies in the fact that I asked Hugh the same question:

"Do you have anything to do with HORSE RACING?" He said No. Then I told him that a horse by the name of Hugh Hefner had been running at Santa Anita, Hollywood Park, Del Mar and other West Coast tracks that year (2002). At that time, I was playing the races daily. I never bet on Hugh Hefner because he was running in claiming races and I liked to play Stakes and Handicap Races.

That year I did well at the tracks, made enough $$$ to buy a new Acura but quit when I bet $4,000 on Cash Run ... and you guessed it, he ran out of the money! With a name like CASH RUN, how could he? Oh well, he was the first horse of 53 horses in a row that failed me!

I'd just thought that I'd pass along this info just so that you would know that I know how to spell Hefner. I had been also working on my updated Profile in which I mentioned the name Howard Hughes ... whom I've never met. It's possible that my mind was on the other HH when I mispelled Hefner.

Oh, for the love of God.

First—he's a published author?? What did he write, *The Book of Moron*?

Second—I wonder if, when he reads his own writing, he has an inexplicable desire to beat himself unconscious.

Third—if you're reading this, Mr. Gasbag: I don't really give a rat's ass whether or not you can spell Hugh Hefner, Howard Hughes, or Mahmoud Ahmadinejad. Please, please never write to me again. I've already destroyed several brain cells reading your drivel.

> i am aroused and very intrested about you ,i prefer the arousing Body and expression and high love ,all day long..i prefer the world of common excitement and love nearly off limits,that thrills and causes high level life enjoyment to both of us ......i would like to see your soul as well ,would like to present you a total change and nymphomanicial lust ,and to open Pandorras box.. i would like to open and get opened a new deep world of real fun,i am an athletic and healthy ,well hung alpha dom ,educated music engineer and architect, and of high experience and unique antique and modern lust-techniques and specials, but i also like to give you sensual well smelling massage with a delicious massage bar or oil ,while lust

torturing,about hours,have ultimative and high drive and looking for the special high drived girl to dive with her into the world of arousing darkness and nymphomanicial lust, causing a fleed of orgasm and drive your pulse to the maximum , ...also intrested in longterm and quality life with you in my large house... ,i am real and expect the same and can show you my all possibilities

(groan) *Nymphomanicial? Fleed??* Oooh...long-term and quality life of lust torturing and diving into arousing darkness and ultimative thrills. Yes, I'm ready to abandon my own life and book the next one-way flight to Germany.

How'r you doing,hope you fine and in good health condition,i read thru your profile and i really loved what i read and thanks for your intrest,My name is xxxxxxx and i hope u would read my profile and find out more about me,i asked myself some questions and give u the answer,can u also answer them and let me know what you think,i would take them one after the other:

So what do you like to do for fun? Your hobbies and interests can reveal a lot about you, and I'd like to learn more. Is there anything special that you're passionate about? I love swimming, taking walks down the park, observing nature, running and walking, i also love cooking and taking walks by the sea side, I'm passionate about a candle lit dinner with i and my partner holding hands together and sharing intimate things about each other. Are you close to your family? I was asking if you're close to your family in the emotional kind of way, but now that I think about it, do they live nearby, too? I'm not really close to my family,cos i don't have one,but each day and night i really miss them all,they don't live nearby. How would you describe your sense of humor? Some people like silly slapstick, while others go for more subtle stuff. What tickles your funny bone? My sense of humor is quite intresting,i'm shy at first but as we get closer i feel free to express my heart desires. What kind of food do you like? Do you have a favorite restaurant? Some like hot and spicy, others prefer comfort food. If you had to pick one type of food, what would you say is your favorite? I love american food and also italian food and most times,i love to cook for myself.I love Mc donalds.I love comfort food. Wow! We could be a match. Would you like to chat online? It seems like we have a lot in common. I'd love to talk to you more and see what develops. What do you think? here till hear from u soon

(reaching for the Advil bottle) This one speaks for itself, people. I have nothing to add.

I'm hardworking Man ,Single , 46 years old , hazel eyes . I love reading ,music ,politics, roses, traveling & computers. You can say that books , music & computer are my real friends . I'm lonely open-minded guy who knows how to care & respect privacies. I need to have a real friend to share thoughts, dreams, fantasies, fetishes, even hard times & as we came to fetishes & fantasies, I have to say that I like some fetishes. I also like 1on1 calls, but I like more romantic nights that full of intimate moments, candles, talking....anything to enjoy my partner doing whatever she wants as long as she can also obey. I for myself has been betrayed by a woman & also men but never lost may faith in people , it is not that wise but just because we cannot live alone or only chose from kind of sex or another ... also I think on the other hand there are lots of faithful & good friends in life .. but it is how & when we meet them or find them .... I'm a man who has that codes which make me suffer in this cruel life, But I will never surrender & I will keep on. well, For all my life I'm looking for real love, I found it but she traveled forever in a way no one can follow but to die... It is ok. Still thought that Love is like a rainbow, beautiful, yet misty.I'm here now just to share & more who knows as I told you I'm still believe that we can be human mirrors so what a luck lady you are you have a mirror for your own (opps) that is only if you accept me with promises of care & understanding going deep inside our souls & mind to see more ... I dream of a woman who can fill my life with her aroma & knows how to serve & to please.So, if you are really someone special who needs a real relation based on , respect , caring & specially passionate .. I'm all yours., just drop some lines telling me more about you.

I'm sorry—what?? I'm afraid your life will have to go on without my aroma. Here's the only line you need—I'm not interested.

hello my dear

i saw your profile and i loved it. the picture is wonderful. but that is not what i am looking for. the girl, woman, lover on my side has to be very pretty inside. that is the only thing that is really important, and what will be very important to me/us.

i am not looking for a sexpartner only, but it is really importantp. i have been inside a RS without sex for 3 years and that almost killed me - REALLY!

i am very open for the most of it but if you are not open enough to live our sexual fantasies, that would be very bad. you must be communicativ, tender,lovely, understanding, inteligent, faithful, submissive and obdient.

let's meet and let's see what happends. i am a good man/dom and it could be your and my dream to go forward and make fantasies come true.

if you are really interested, than please write me to with your contact adress - best would be a mess anger-adress.

you should know, that i am very sexual and have a good sexdrive when i am attracted to my sub and have found my real sub, but not just "fuck". qualitiy is more important then quantity. but i also love to pleasure my partner like she does it to me. with feelings it is more beautyful that just without.

i love my partner to be more sub, sluty, devoted and submissive. i am looking for my all-in-one-girl-sub. the bdsm-part is a part of my life - not my whole life - but very important.

you should love to dress yourself sexy on my side. best thing would be, when you have a fable for skirts, sexy shirts/blouse, black(pvc-latex), leather, high heels or boots. i really will admire her for that and will take good care, protect and support her.

be sure, i don't care any distance, because when we got the connection, we will see where the way goes and leads us.

i am single and i am open to relocate you or myself when it is necessary, when i have found the right sub. i don't care where my sub is form and how long it needs to meet here as long as we are in contact. but the domination is a part of me - and your devotion is a gift to me, that i will respect and admire.

i am not a player or a time waster - i met to many on this site. i had a sub, but she was busy all the time and the business was more important - i had to accept that.

i pormise, when you answer you won't be disappointed. Kiss

Whaddaya mean, you're not a time-waster? You've already wasted several precious minutes of my life that I'll never get back. If you're a dom, why do you lower-case your I's? And finally—if you're willing to relocate me, would you relocate my boyfriend too? Please let me know on mess anger...uh, Messenger. Thanks much, dear.

It seems he doesn't keep track of his recipients, because here he is again:

hello my dear

i saw your profile and i love also the picture is wonderful. what i am looking for in my all-in-one-girl is a lover, best friend, my ..... you must be sexy, hot dressed in heels/boots, skirts, communicativ, tender,lovely, understanding, inteligent, faithful, ... and a sort of submissive and obdient. i am a good man/dom and it could be your and my dream to go forward and make fantasies come true.

> i really will admire her for the devotion and will take good care, protect and support her. be sure, i don't care any distance, because when we got the connection, we will see where the way goes and leads us. i am single and i am open to relocate you or myself when it is necessary, when i have found the right sub. i am not a player or a time waster - i met to many on this site.

Don't go updating your passport just yet, my dear.

Oh, and lest you think that these form letters only occur on the kink sites, think again. I received this next gem on Facebook!

> Good day and how are you doing? Am [deleted] from England, am a single, honest, kind, caring, loyal and God fearing.I came across your profile on facebook and am interested in getting acquainted with you deeply.It will be wonderful experience to have a personality like you.Am single and have been longing for a responsible woman to make my life more complete.
>
> How i wish i live to appreciate you.hope to have an interesting moment to share with you.From the dept of my heart i say to you....you are wonderful.kindly get back to me soon.

Hmmm. Isn't "getting acquainted deeply" an oxymoron? Nice to know your heart has its own department. Talk about compartmentalizing.

> Sir found your profile quite interesting. It appears W/we share several interests. Particularly, your ability to express your desires.
>
> I'm a well-educated secure professional who has been in the Lifestyle for over 20 years. That experience allows ME to understand MY partner's needs and desires so that I can fully "explore" and "expand" them.
>
> To find a person that truly understands MY desires is quite rare. In reading your profile, I see someone who possibly shares MY interests and is compatible with MY way of life. Importantly, I see a person who appreciates the wonder of this unique Lifestyle.

Explore this: 1. Referring to yourself in the third person is pretentious. 2. MY, MY, MY…not too full of yourself, are you? 3. My profile had absolutely nothing in it that was compatible with your "Lifestyle." Admit it—you were just looking at my ass. 4. You're boring. Fuck off.

Here's another ME ME ME guy:

> I would like to get to know you better. If you are interested in Me as well, then I would begin by asking how open minded you are. The more open minded, the better.
>
> you may find yourself sending Me photos from your phone as I instruct you perform humiliating things for Me. you might also write Me naughty, filthy stories based on your

fantasies, or on the real life slutty things you do.

I am looking for submissive pen pals who enjoys verbal and physical humiliation.

I am a real Dom, and have little patience for silly games. If you are serious and willing to consider giving yourself (online) to Me?

...then contact Me.

Forgive me for the following bit of opinionated snark, but puh-leeeeze, who do these guys and their capital Me think they are?

As you know, I don't answer these messages, but this time I was irresistibly driven, because I was just so damned irked by this guy's ego. So I wrote back:

"Good lord. Get over yourself. Try actually reading a woman's profile before you send her this über-Dom drivel."

He didn't reply to that. I'm devastated.

FORMER ROCK STAR Not really a rock superstar , but worked with some great groups including "Alice Cooper" and "Earth , Wind and Fire" , I was a great "jouneyman" musician , not a great songwriter , and a quality , but not unique voice. As with most musicans , incredible sexual adventures , which brought me to this world.. Now , a successful film/tv agent. A different approach.. hopefully , successful. This site , and all "meeting sites" are difficult , in very different ways , for men and women. You get massive hits and emails , and men get limited responses. Perhaps my candor will work. This is all absolutely true. I'm 59...attractive , work out daily , in good shape (not a hunk , but when naked , in front of the mirror...I'm happy). Dominant , and when being that , a great Dom. In the past few years , I have "switched" and do find it interesting , but , no less the "Dom". A simple proposal. Drinks or dinner. If nothing else , some great , intelligent conversation. Perhaps about this world , or life , or love. My profile is all true...and I promise you'll find me charming , respectful , and fun...Sincere Thanks

Ooooooh! Earth, Wind and Fire! I can feel my panties dampening already! First, you say you're 59 but your profile says you're 62. Second, you use way too damn many commas and a space before each of them is unnecessary. And third, ever wonder exactly why you get limited responses? Give that a think next time you're standing in front of the mirror naked.

First let ME clarify that Ww/e have the time and resources to travel and be where we want when we want. We can travel nationally if we feel the person warrants it. Seriously searching we have the time to make the effort to meet truly serious people. PICS ON PROFILE.

Secondly, we can devote large amounts of time to training, play and lifestyle travel with you. If you are inexperienced, brand new, or live a distance, it is not a problem. We travel to you, if need be and in those cases where it has worked well we have you travel with us on kinky holidays, trips and to lifestyle resorts. If you are new you will be safe, learn at your own pace and be shown all that you need to know to be active in a safe way. For the more experienced we look for a different experience of intense edge play and intense scenes and complex play with larger equipment and scenes such as abduction, interrogation, play rape, forced use and humiliation.

Intense and commanding, educated and worldly, a skilled teacher, We seek primarily a fem sub/slave or couple to pursue the joys and pleasures of bdsm and the erotic arts. Both are fit, attractive, very creative, kinky, sexually on fire, and bring a very firm hand to training and discipline, but open and clear in our desires and wants. I have a great deal of experience, am very visual, a leather lover, enjoy complex "scenes", and expert with MY tools and toys. We are a long term lifestyle Dom/sub couple and will take you sexually and mentally where you have not gone before.

We believe in safe, sane and have a strong need to dominate and use you in endless ways. I have done MY "homework" and know the power of the mind, understand submission and know well the role of a Master in the care and development of the submissive/slave mind. It's not just about kinky sex, but about the blend of sex, control, submission and emotional need. The best have it in their DNA. She is bisexual, skilled and polished in the art of slavery and submission.

We have a full life being a successful professionals, direct and honest, passionate about life and living to the fullest. I am lean, passionate, strong hands and sexually insatiable using the body and mind for intense mind fucks. She is multi orgasmic, long legged and a lean blonde slut. I have trained and owned slaves in the past and am a skilled and patient teacher of "newbies" as well as those who are seasoned.

I enjoy, practice and excel at many fetishes including long sessions of bdsm, rope play, anal play, electric, rope and whip and flogger and a wide range of mental fetish play, sexual D/s, and adult exploration. I push boundaries including edge play, but take you there safely and back. I am active in the San Diego and LA bdsm communities, frequent the dungeons and private play parties and discreet meets and socials.

What a pity that I wasted my time reading all of this, when you so clearly didn't read a word of my profile.

I could go into all the reasons why what you've written to me is so, so inappropriate for my scene dynamic, but I don't have all weekend. Oh, and I prefer to call myself "experienced." Saying I'm "seasoned" makes it sound like I have 11 secret herbs and spices on my ass.

I have come to the end of the gasbaggery. And just when we were having so much fun, too. Next up: what's going to be my personal favorite chapter: People who need a tutorial on how to give a compliment!

THE BACKHANDED COMPLIMENT

Another question for those of you who know me well—what do I love, kids? Right! Compliments with age qualifiers (which, in essence, negate the compliment).

I entered the scene relatively late in life; probably not super late for my generation, but certainly a lot older than the current generations who now grow up with the Internet and have access to all things spanking without having to sneak around or ask embarrassing questions. I was 38 when I "came out," and I didn't shoot my first video until I was 42. And I kept on shooting all through my 40s and well into my 50s. Due to a combination of exercise, sun-shunning, and plain old good luck, I've managed to age fairly gracefully so far. So apparently, people are surprised when they find out my real age, which I've never hidden. At the time of this writing, I'm 55 years old.

I realize that the folks in this chapter most likely meant well. However—and if I had a dollar for every time I've stated this, I could retire now—if you tell a woman she looks good *for her age*, that is not a compliment. Why add the qualifier? Would you tell a 25-year-old woman that she looks good for her age? Of course not. She looks good, period.

When I hear, "Wow, you look great for your age," I also hear this, quietly implied: "Wow! You're so damn old, you should be looking like a dried-out hag by now! What a surprise that you still look good!" And yet, no matter how many times I've tried to set people straight on this, I get these types of comments time and time again.

And then there are the ones who aren't necessarily complimenting, but they feel this urgent need to mention my age anyway. Words like "older" and "mature" are sprinkled in. I get a fair amount of this, too.

You'll see, with all the following.

"Its been awhile since I've had an older piece off pussy."

Older piece of pussy? Thank you so much. So, just how does an older piece differ from a younger piece? Do you have to blow off the dust first?

UR SO FUCKN SEXY IS IT WRONG OF ME THAT I WANNA FUCK A 49 YEAR OLD HOTTIE

Hmmmm. No, it's not wrong, per se. But it would have been nice if you'd put it a little less crudely. And stop shouting at me.

I didn't reply to the above, so a few days later, I got this from the same gentleman:

Why wont u talk to me u dont like young dick? i got pics

Young Dick? Wasn't that a Mel Brooks movie about the life of Richard Nixon?

Erica, you sure do a good job of keeping yourself in shape for your age!

Why, thank you! I do try. You know, if you buy Geritol by the case, you get a discount. And I do try to keep my walker nicely polished.

YOU ARE THE HOTTEST WOMAN I HAVE EVER SEEN AT 50! GOOD FUCKING JOB!!!!!

(sigh). Thank you...I think. But I owe it all to exercise, dieting, and not bearing children. Fucking had nothing to do with it.

i hope i can find myself a beautiful ladie like you that will share my pasion for spanking untill we are both wrinklie oldies babe
ps you still looking very hot hun

You'd better make sure that ladie doesn't have a pasion for good spelling. (rolling eyes)

eRICA - UR LOOKING VERY GOOD FOR 50 YEARS OLD, congradulations.

How many things can be wrong with just one sentence? Forget the age reference; that's been done to death. But maybe the old saying is true; too much masturbation causes blindness. Don't people look at what they're writing? Can't they see that they have the CAPS button engaged, and their caps and lower case are coming out ass backwards?

you do have a nice ass for 50 and thats comming from a blk mans point of view lol

Oh, my goodness. How wrong is this—let me count the ways. The ubiquitous age reference. The

62

misspellings. The lack of proper punctuation. Plus, what does his being a black man have to do with anything? Are black men's points of view different from white men's? Is this a reference to the well-worn cliché about how black men prefer woman with more junk in the trunk (i.e., a big booty)? So, is he trying to tell me I have a big butt?? (shaking head) Why am I trying to psychoanalyze this? I'm getting a headache.

> wow hey seen u on a friends profile and i must say u are an extremly older female and i was wondering if u liked younger guys

Geeeeez!! It's not enough that I'm considered an older woman—now I'm an *extremely* older woman?? Yes, I like younger guys. But if I'm extremely old to you, then you must be a child. Go back to your sandbox.

> I will never in my life beleive that ass is 50 years old.

You better beleive [sic] it, baby. My ass is well preserved. I massage it every night with Oil de Formaldehyde Beauty Creme.

> i like older lades i holp your not mad

(sigh) No, this was not written by a five-year-old child, but a 30-year-old man. Can we please observe a moment of silence, in mourning for our educational system?

you have a very attractive seating area, mature, which responsd nicely to traditional attention.

Seating area?? What the hell do I have back there, an auditorium? And there's that damned "mature" word again. Yeah, I got your mature right here, pal.

hi erica wow your beautiful so so gorgeous marry me . ill date you the rest of my life . your the sexest 50 year old lady i ever seem . please marry me . im in love with you. keeping smileing sugar.

Thank you, dear, I'm flattered. But if God forbid I should ever enter the dysfunctional institution of marriage, it will have to be with someone who knows the difference between your and you're, seem and seen, ill and I'll, etc. Not that I'm picky or anything.

50 yrs and u look like that dammm baby sry to say this but i just got this massive hardon im like wtf woooooooooooooooooow have a great day what a babe

Yeah, right—he's not at all *sry* to say it. Why do these guys feel the burning need to share their state of tumescence with me? (Oh, look it up. It's near turgidity.)

U HAVE A SMOKIN BODY FOR A LADY YOUR AGE!!

(sigh) I may be old, but I'm not deaf. There's no need to SHOUT. And you know, one exclamation point gets the point across. For extra emphasis, you can use two. But using a hundred of them is redundant.

> aY 50 YOUR STILL LOOKING GOOD AND VERY SPANKABLE, TOO BAD YOUR NOWHERE NEAR HERE.

Oh, yes, too bad. I'm sobbing into my Wheaties over it.

> just wanted to say youre one hot 50 year old. i hope my woman (whatever woman im with then i mean) has a bod like her at your age!

OK, this makes no sense. You hope your woman has a bod like her? Of course she'll have a bod like her. Who else's bod would she have?

Side note: This guy's profile says "I love red asses in the air!" Hmmm. Are these asses attached to anything (like a person), or are they disembodied floating ass balloons?

> You sure have a great bare bottom for a 50 year old.I would love anything to spank it.I am in very good shape I run marathons very little fat.

> my wife the one who got me it to it but with her I must be careful since she is a small woman.she loves it when she still can feel it the next day.

of course she spanks me to at first I was not ok with that but you know how demending some woman are so I gave it.it was great.so all I can say I wish I could know you but live so far away.my wife did it because it tought us a lesson on trust.
weird right.

"weird right"…you're not kidding, cookie. Good grief. No, actually, I have no idea—how *demending* are some woman? (That was rhetorical—please don't flood me with comments enlightening me!)

I get extremely turned on at the thoughts of being with a horny wet mature lady – lying on satin sheets with her stroking my hard 10 inches.

He's seeking "mature wild women"—probably needless to say, he's a lot younger than I am. I dunno, call me crazy, but I just don't find "horny wet mature lady" all that flattering. Plus, I think he suffers from delusion. Either that or he challenged with numbers and measurements. Perhaps he needs to bone up on those.

HEY ERICA ARE YOU A SINGLE FEMALE DO YOU LIKE OLDER MEN YES OR KNOW CAN YOU SEND ME A NEW MESSAGE MY NAME IS XXXXXXX IM A 38 YEAR OLD MALE WITH A NICE BODY ON ME YOU DO LOOK GOOD FOR YOUR AGE

Yes or know?? And just why is he asking me if I like older men, when he's 38? And there's that "good for your age" crack again. Newsflash, guys. Backhanded compliments do not count as spankings!

So I deleted the message, and five minutes later, I got this:

HEY ERICA CAN YOU SEND ME A NEW MESSAGE I LOVE OLDER WOMEN THAT ARE 51 YEARS OLD

Wow...not just older women, but 51-year-old women! Not 50, not 52. Does that mean that after my next birthday, he won't love me anymore?

for 50 your man has a nice butt to spank

Hey! How do you know my man has a nice butt??

Here's one I got from a 25-year-old. It was a rarity, because I actually replied to it; I just couldn't let this one stand without making a statement, in hopes that I would enlighten this person.

so whats it like to still be spanked at your age?

That scraping sound you hear is me grinding my teeth. Here's what I sent back to him, verbatim:

"(sigh) Well, you know, I have to be careful. If I get too excited, it throws my pacemaker off. And it's a lot harder to go OTK these days with all this arthritis—I prefer men to bend me over my walker. Oh, and it's really embarrassing when they pull down my Depends."

Sends a clear message, don't you think? And yet, this was his next message:

your cute lol. so really what is like to still be spanked?

Say it with me, boys and girls—clueless!! No, I didn't answer him.

For a 51 year old woman, I must say you are amazingly attractive.

(sigh) Must you? Really?
Oh, and your sentence structure blows. Are *you* a 51-year-old woman?

is that really your ass! the ass of a 51 year old woman? wow!

Nahh, don't be ridiculous. Of course it isn't mine. I stole it. Everyone knows that a 51-year-old woman's ass looks like soggy pancakes.
Someone asked me recently, regarding the age comments, "what's the big deal?" Well, the big deal is that it bugs the crap out of me. Is that enough of a reason?

i hope it isnt rude but ur really sexy for a woman your age

Eh...rude? I guess not. Stupid? You betcha.

cant believe you are 52 with that firm ass and pretty face

At least this one noticed my face. But please, for the millionth time, why is it so unbelievable? I know, I know. Give it up. They won't change. But it's still makes me feel better to bitch about it.

> i generaly date woman older than me theres many reasons for that.i luv the matureity and nolage and sefistication.and in generaly atracted to older woman since i was a teenager.thats a nuff about me.

Yes, that's more than a nuff. Can someone please enlighten me on how someone who is this illiterate can function? I really am in need of this nolage.

> omg i don't wanna be rude but are you really 52? u r freakin hott!

Why is it whenever someone says that they don't mean to do or be whatever, they then proceed to do what they just said they don't mean? (And if you could follow that, props to you.)

> i never thought a woman like you could have this really tight, succulent ass.

A woman like me? Hmmm…how many guesses do I get, about what he means by that? Never mind, I only need one guess. He might as well have said, "I never thought a woman as old as you would have an ass that doesn't sag down to the backs of her knees."

> Your in good shape for your vintage

Vintage?? I'm a freaking wine now?

> You don't look a d day over 45 are u sure your
> age is correct. :)

Now wait just a damn minute. When did I get so freaking old that 45 is a compliment? (insert bursting-into-tears emoticon here.) And excuse me, but D-Day dates back to World War II. That is before my vintage, thank you very much.

> hy. if you wanna be spanked by a young stud
> thats interested in older women let me know ;)
> im 5 miles away from you and free to c u at any
> time
> p.s. im looking for older women ;)

Yeah. I got that. Older women. Thank you. And no, thank you. P.S....*hy*??

> would you concider erotic emails with me?
> Sorry to be blut but I just love older women and
> My wife enjoys reading them.

Your wife enjoys reading older women? (scratching head)

> You dont look 54! more like 24! omg how do
> you stay so young? I would love to get to no
> you!

Well, of course I don't look 54. I'm 52. And you can stop sucking up—I know good and well that even on my best day with the best lighting and the best makeup, I do not look 24.

I looked at this guy's SpankFinder profile. His spanking preferences are Roll Play and Domestic Decipline. And his hobbies include (spelling verbatim) Musiems, Driveing his 62 Linkcon, and—wait for it—Quatum Physics!

(How does one do Roll Play, anyway? Are butter and jam involved?)

> I am looking for someone younger but just wanted to stop by and tell you how much I enjoyed your profile.

Uh huh. And to tell me that I'm too old. By the way, you're in your 60s and you're looking for someone younger than I am? Good luck with that.

> Hey, you know of anyone in there 20's who might be interested?

Interested in…what, exactly? Someone who doesn't know how to spell "their"? And do I look like a spanking broker to you?

> Just got to say your pic is really nice. Even dispute the age diffrence it turns me on.

Just had to bring up the age diffrence [sic], didn't you. Tsk. There's no disputing that you're an idiot.

> Hello! At your age, you still do have some nice ass to be slapped. My hands are itching.

Then scratch them, stupid.

ooolala babe your are absolutely stunning for
52 would like to spank you every min i get if
you let me

Everybody sing! "Ga, ga, oooh la LAAA!" Ooops.
Sorry. Got a little carried away there, channeling
Lady Gaga. Anyway...No, I won't let you, babe.

lovely pussy
u are amazing at 52

Yeah, yeah, yeah. I'm a walking miracle.

wats up how u doin sexxy u look verry good 4
ur age

Get lost, Junior.

That's one great ass you have there Erica. You
look PHENOMENAL for 53!

Oh, now I'm PHENOMENAL. I suppose at 54, I'll
be MIRACULOUS, and by 55, I'll be OTHER-
WORLDLY. (rolling eyes)

Nice ass for 53!

(sigh) Oh, fuck off. (sorry, but if he's not going to be
imaginative, then neither am I.)

i wanna give you the best panties for an older
woman award :]

Well, thank you! I'm honored. I owe it all to Granny
Spanx.

72

It is hard to believe your bottom look like this at age 53!

Oh, I give up. You got me. That picture you saw is one I stole from a 25-year-old.

Wow that is a lovely bottom. Especially for your age (I bet you hate hearing that).

You'd win that bet. And yet, you said it anyway, asshat.

Received this on FetLife:

Love your awesome 50 something petite build

He then went on to invite me to join his group and provided a link. I clicked on it and was taken to the group "Skinny Thin Sluts."

I said no, thanks. I already belong to "Slender Lightweight Hussies."

Well, may I say you look fabulously sprightly for your age.

No, you may not. Sprightly?? Who am I, Granny Clampett?

Lady for 55 you have the best damn ass Ive ever seen. Come live with me and let me stroke and spank that ass for the rest of our lives!!!

Honey, if I came to live with you, the rest of our lives would be very brief indeed. Trust me on this one.

Oh, thank God. I've finally completed the ageist section. And now if you will please excuse me, I'm going to have a cocktail of warm milk and Metamucil and go to bed. If I can haul this old carcass upright tomorrow, I'll write about people who think I'm deaf.

Enough with the Yelling

What's worse than an offensive, stupid message? An offensive, stupid message written in ALL CAPS.

In general, writing in all caps is discouraged. It's considered the written version of shouting, it's hard to read, and it's lazy to boot. How difficult is it to use a Shift key? A word or two for emphasis, or to depict an excited utterance, is one thing. But entire sentences and paragraphs are off-putting.

So I'm sure it will come as no surprise that I've received quite a few missives that holler at me.

I WILL SPANK YOUR ASS

Um, no, you won't. You can shout all you want; it's not happening.

ILIKE I LIKE SWEETIE DAMM VERY SEXY BEOTIFULL HAY SWEETIE ILIKE TO GET TO KNOW YOU .MABE I COULD COME AND GIVE YOU A WONDERFULL MASSAGE ITS SOUNDS CRAZY BUT IAM VERY SEXY 29 YO YOUYNG FULL OFF ENERGUY 6/3 TALL 189 LB BLACK HERE GREEN EYS VERY ATRACTIVE..

He's right about one thing—it sounds crazy.

Tell me—just how tall is six-thirds tall? Is *energuy* an amalgam of energetic and guy? Black here? Black where? What exactly is the crazy part—that he's 29? That he has green eys....er, eyes?

And why is he shouting at me? Is he going to keep on yelling while he gives me a massage? That's not very relaxing.

WANNA DO A LITTLE I SPANK U, U SPANK ME VIA THE OVER THE INTERNET.

The long answer? First, stop shouting at me. Second, I do not top, for the umpteenth time. And third, I don't play "via the over the" Internet. It's the real thing or nothing, for this girl. The short answer? Bugger off.

This next guy started with upper and lower case, at least. Still illegible, though.

nothing like a sexy butt to spanked i think a mirror so u can watch yourself get it good hands only (sorry)

Say it with me, kids—WTF?? Can someone please interpret this for me?

As if that weren't enough, this morning, I got this gem, from the same person:

SHADOWLANE WHAT A NAME WANT TO MEET NOT FOR PAIN JUST TO SPANK JUST FOR FUN AM DESCREET ONE ON ONE KIND OF SHY AT THE START HOLDING HANDS IN THE DARK CARRESS YOUR BACK CUP YOUR BUNS TENDER KISS BUT WERE NOT DONE SOFTER KISS FOR QUITE SOME TIME THEN SOME MORE NOW YOUR MINE PUT U DOWN TO MY KNEE

> PANTIES SLIDE TO YOUR FEET LEG TOGETHER
> TELL U WHAT SPARE NO ROD SLAP UR BUTT!

Hmmm. You know, I'll bet this guy spent all week thinking about how he could outperform his last note. "I know! I'll make it longer, even more stupid, and I'll put it in ALL CAPS TO BE REALLY ANNOYING!"

This one is from a 17-year-old:

> HEY CUTE LOVE YOURE PICS MAKES ME GET
> ALL HORNY WHEN I SEE THEM..LOL..HI

Uh... shouldn't you be playing with an XBox or something, kiddo? Please, please don't be looking at me. I am nearly three times your age. That's just wrong. And will people ever learn to stop typing in ALL CAPS? No wonder there is an obesity epidemic in this country, if we are too lazy to even press a Shift key.

> ID LOVE TO SPANK YOUR PRETTY ASS THEN RUB
> IT DOWN WITH OIL WHILE YOU TEND TO ME.

Excuse me? While I tend to you? Think again, pal. Wait—scratch that. Think, period. It might be new to you, but you'll get used to it.

> YOU HAVE BEEN A BAD SLUT AND YOU NEED
> TO BE SPANKED AND FUCKED PROPER..

I'm so sorry. I'll try to be a *good* slut next time.

Received this one during the Bush administration, hence my comment:

NASTY SUGAR DADDY FUCKING..2ND ATTEMPT! Have a proposition 4 u! RING ME: [phone number deleted] HI THERE! KISSSSS NEED TO TUCH U IN ALL UR SECRET PLACES INVADE U IN ALL UR PRIVATE SPACES. TASTE ALL UR FORBIDDEN PLEASURES TUCH U IN WAYS OTHER MEN HAVE NOT! THRU EXTENDED PSYCH AND MENTAL /PHYSICAL FOREPLAY ..IMAGINE UR VAGINA AS A GOLDEN MAGICAL DOOR..THE HEAD OF MY COCK AS A GIANT KNOCKER WANT TO POKE PROD SEARCH ALL UR DAMP SPOTS WITH THE TIP OF THE HEAD OF MY COCK--MAKE CERTAIN I HAV A WARM WELCUM MB4 I ENTER--MAKE UWANT TO TELL ME YES I WANT U TO LOVE ME YES I WANNA ACCEPT UR COCK AS THE MASTER OF ALL MY PUSSYS'S PLEASURES! instant chemistry erection seeing ur profile..hard not b/c i wanna get off--but b/c i wana please u with this hardness.the sounds of our juices mixing together--can make u want this 400% huungry greedy eager for urgent penetrating lov e-ing

I don't know where to begin with this one. This is beyond shame. This can't be real. No one could be this stupid. Oh, wait…look who has been in office for the past eight years. Never mind.

What interesting imagery. My privates are a magical golden door, and he's a giant knocker. Is this what they mean by "knocked up"?

And just what the hell are the "sounds of juices mixing"? How do you hear juices mix?

How does one measure hunger in percentages? Fascinating.

U ARE A HOTIE I WOULD LOVE TO KEEP U UP
MISS LOL :)

What's a hotie? Well, at least he called me Miss, not Ma'am.

THIS IS XXXX IM 33 6'0 BRN HAIR HAZEL GREEN
EYES TAN 225LBS, U LOOK STUNNING, I GOTTA
SPANK UR TIGHT ASS, XXX-XXX-XXXX, LETS TALK
I WOULD LOVE TO HEAR UR VOICE, UR
PERFECT, AND ON THE RIGHT SIDE OF 50 U
LOOK INCREDIBLE

Oh, yeah, I'm rushing to the phone. Sorry, honey, you want to spank the wrong animal. Go spank your monkey instead.

YOU LOOK SO FUCKING SEXY AND IF YOU WILL
PLEASE GIVE ME YOUR EMAIL ADDRESS I WILL
SEND YOUR SEXY ASS PICS OF MY DICK

Wow, he said please! Watch me fall all over myself in my haste to write back to him and get those pictures.

SUPER SEXY MS LADY CHECKOUT BOTTEMS UP.
PAGE. TL MAYBE I CAN GET A ASS SHOT OF U
ON THERE I REALLY NEED YOUR SEXINESS. CAN

I GET A ASS SHOT? TEXT ME [phone #
deleted]....

Get your own sexiness; you can't have mine. Let's
see—he used all caps and the A word, twice. The
only offense he forgot was to make a reference to my
age. I guess he had to say ass, since he apparently
can't spell bottom.

HEY HW U DOIN U REAL CUTE WATS UR NAME

My name is Erica. Your name is apparently not
Einstein.

GOOD EVE ERICA MY U LOOK SIMPLY AMAZING
IN UR PICS ..WOULD JUST LUV TA BEND U
OVER.AFTER A GREAT CANDLELITE DINNER AND
BURP YA MY BABY.

You want to do *what*?? I'm not your baby, you
moron. Get away from me before I spit up on you.
And stop yelling. It hurts my baby ears.
　　Didn't reply, of course. And then he wrote:

was just wondering.that.is it most ppl that get
nice comments never respond if they have over
12 friends l.o.l..sick and tired of typing fr no
reason.

What he'd written before—that was a nice
comment? Seriously? He's really disgruntled because
I didn't respond to his desire to burp me? (shaking
head)

I AM PERFECT FOR YOU LOVER! SERIOUSLY I HAVE AN INSATIABLE ASS FETISH THAT WOULD AMAZE YOU AND I AM ALWAYS IN NEED OF A NEW BOTTOM.WHENEVER-WHEREVER I AM ADDICTED TO LICKING,SUCKING,AND FUCKING A NICE ASS LIKE YOURS.PLEASE MESSAGE ME ASAP SINCE WE LIVE SO CLOSE.I PROMISE YOU'LL BE PLEASED.

OK, first—DON'T YELL. Second, not in a million years would I be your lover. Third, you mention every possible thing that can be done to an ass, except the one thing I want, which is spanking. Oh, wait. There is one more thing that can be done to an ass—kicking it out the cyber door.

I wonder if people with insatiable ass fetishes grow up to be proctologists?

A week or two later, same guy:

I HAVE AN INSATIABLE ASS FETISH. I'M SEEKING A PLAYDATE-PARTNER.I'M VERY DESCREET AND I LOVE OLDER WOMEN AND ANYTHING TO DO WITH THE FEMALE ASS.SO MESSAGE ME BACK ASAP.

I guess he still hasn't found his dream ass. Amazing.

HI, WE HAVE CHATTED BEFORE U R SOOOOOO RIGHT I WANT U TO CUM 4 ME THEN I KNOW I SPANKED YOU AND U LOVED THE SCENE---ITS ABOUT MAKING MY PARTNER HAPPY WITH A RED RED ASS---U IN SUN-DRESS IN PARK WITH ME---THONG PANTIES ON SO I LIFT DRESS TAKE YOUR SANDAL + PADDLE U WHEN JOGGERS

RUN BY MMMMMM BET I COULD MAKE U COMMMMM MORE MORE LOVE PUBLIC PLAY WITH BEAUTIFIL WOMAN LIKE YOU MMMM NOW IM HARD---GO GET MY BELT YOUNG LADY--GET IN CORNER AND WAIT 4 YOUR SPANKING---HOLD UP THAT DRESS NOW U BAAAAAD LIL GIRL. MMMMMM LOVE DADDY.

Stop hollering, you moron. Actually, stop talking and stop typing while you're at it. I'm afraid you have "commmmming" confused with vomiting.

Last but not least—Return to sender, address unknown:

HEY Ally WAT R U DOIN BABY YES U NEED A SPANKIN I NEED TO SPANK U BABY BOO IM SO HORNY AND HARD BC OF U

Who the hell is Ally? Go find her and leave me alone.

I do apologize to any of my readers who suffer from migraines. No doubt this chapter brought one on. Go take an Imitrex and come back for more fun when you feel better.

PASS THE BRAIN BLEACH

Alas, no such product exists. But this chapter will make you wish that it did.

Granted, all the messages in this book are objectionable in one way or another. However, this chapter's entries are especially vile. I understand that the Internet affords a degree of anonymity, plus some folks feel like we have some sort of intimacy happening because they've watched me on video or read my writing. Common sense would dictate that they'd know this pseudo-intimacy doesn't exist...but we all know that, if this book is any indication, common sense is as rare as hen's teeth. Take a deep breath, make sure your stomach is settled, and join me in an exploration of explicit filth, wayward wankers, and way too damn much information.

> I would like to put a firm hand on that bueatiful rear end.Some things about me. I had a prostate promblem so my dick dosnt work so good. That is way i am looking for new ways of entainment.

(groaning) Can you say TMI, kiddies?

> I like to warm up a sexy ass before I gently fuck it. If anal is a hard limit, I may allow you to give me a nice blowjob as a reward for all the work I put into "tanning your ass."

Did I say anything about wanting sex, anal or otherwise? And you'll allow me to give you a blowjob? Excuse me, pal, but spanking me, or any other woman, isn't work—it's a privilege.

> hiya sexc....
> think u r hot...wished we lived closer...
> god u make me hard...at work now, looking at u...
> yum!

Is it really that difficult to type y-o-u instead of u? How lazy are these people? I suppose I should make allowances, considering a lot of these guys are typing with one hand, but still.

> i'm looking for a slim and naughty and submissive hairless girl
> you may request what you want me to do with you –
> but you shall be ready to do what i want you to do!
> 1st: your intimate area shall be shaved totally
> 2nd: you shall be naked at home anytime
> 3rd: you like to be cummed
> 4th: you want to be filled at all
> i will admit three claims from you - after you admitted my requests and will reclaim my following requests:
> - you'll never wear any kind of underwear - like slip or bra
> - you'll shave your intimate area every day totally
> - you'll always wear tops that let your bellybutton free and visible

- you'll look at men first their balls ... and decide further
- you'll welcome ME anytime and anywhere being naked with a neverlasting blow until i cum your face
if you will agree to all of this we will be friends and have a very good time - for sure!

I guess I'm out from the start, since I'm not hairless. The Sinead O'Connor look isn't a good one for me.

hey baby how are you?
do u like masturbate cam 2 cam?
i like that so much
and i like ur pics baby
pls add me
i wait for u darling
couse you are realllly so sexy babe
i m sure u ll enjoy so much when i m doing somthings for u on cam baby
now i m looking ur pics and wanking
but pls dont angry to me that s not my fault...
you are very beautifull :))

I'm not completely naive. I realize that Internet pictures are often wank fodder. But really, do I have to hear about it? Who is this Cam person, and why do people like to do so many things on him/her?

very bad i want to spank you.
i want to lick you
i want to eat you...
yes i am horny...lol
write back

Really? You're horny? I never would have guessed. Very bad you write, Yoda. Now be a good little wanker and beat it.

> Nothing beats grabbing a freshly spanked and bright red ass and pulling it back as you have anal sex.

Is it just me, or is this way too personal a comment? I mean, I don't even know this guy's name, and already I know he's a buttbanger.

> You are an amazing Goddess (who deserves to be spanked and, if the truth be told, really fucked hard in your ass - the way I do my wife most nights of the week).

I'm sure your wife loves having perfect strangers privy to that knowledge. Tell me—does she return the favor, or is that not possible, since your head is already up there?

This next one baffled me—it was posted to a picture of just me, not me with anyone else:

> i want to spank both of you hard then put my big dick up your asses

(looking around) Are there two of me? God help the world! And, do tell, how do you put your dick up two asses at once? Is it bifurcated? Double your pleasure...

> hey baby wanna trade nudes...i know im only 15 but i have a huge dick and the pics to prove it

Young man, what did your mother tell you about showing your penis to strangers? Now stop that wanking in front of your computer and go to bed—it's a school night.

I get the biggest hard-on from spanking a nice butt. Do you find this to be normal?

Nope, you're a freak. Get help. What am I, a doctor? How should I know what's normal—I don't have one of those thingamajigs you boys have to deal with.

after you get that gorgeous ass spanked again id so love to get my tounge to work on it ...and in it....damn it's such a turn on...like, your whole body fantastic...but that god damn, love ot eat it with some whipped cream and nutella chocolate spread ASS...wow!!...

Wow, indeed. Some of these people make my brain ache. And my stomach churn. Nutella??

you certain got my cock hard:) what are you wearing right now?

What am I wearing? You've got to be kidding me—people still ask that? I thought "what are you wearing" went out with "Hey baby, what's your sign?"

hey my queen...
look,,for how long i should resist ur beauty..uhh????im dyin to spank u soo hard

and make u sit on my face for hours!! ohhh...&
suck & lick ur feet for years..i really want u!!? y
dont u come? Plzzzzz
i love ur age babe...wanna love u!!

We are not amused. Your Queen has spoken. We do
not sit on faces, we sit on thrones.

Damn... I love a good blogger. I stiffened right
up.

I'm so happy I could help. Read my blog and you
can save a fortune on Viagra.

You"re just plain beautiful.You could tell most
men to bend over and let you fuck them with a
strapon,and most would let you.I would.Would
you do that if you had a chance?

First, in case anyone is wondering, the answer is
NO. Not him, or any other man. I'm the one who's
supposed to bend over, remember? (for a spanking,
dammit! Get your minds out of the gutter.) Good
grief. Second, really, there has to be another way to
express to a woman that she's attractive. Finally, one
word, honey: spacebar.

The following ten entries all have the same thing
in common: The writers clearly paid no attention to
my profile and my fetish preferences. I'm not a
Domme, I'm purely into spanking (not breast play),
and I don't have any mother/son fantasies. But you
wouldn't know it, reading these:

hi i was browsing profiles i have a fantasy
question hope it dont offend u or upset u if u

was my mom and u wanted me to try on girls clothes for one day how would u convince me to do it

If I were your mother, I'd shoot myself. And spanking is my kink, not dressing up boys in girls' clothing, so I haven't the faintest notion how to answer this question. Why do people assume that because you're into one kink, you're an expert on all of them? Anyway, go play, sweetie. Don't get your dress dirty, or Mama will have to put you in the corner. (Ack, I just squicked myself, writing that.)

hi i am a baby slave and have to wear my diapers or mommy spanks me! my mommy gina is my wife and i am not aloud to go pee setting up if i am out of my diapers

Not my fetish, dude. I think your mommy, or your wife, or whoever the hell she is, needs to keep you away from the computer. At least until you're in big-boy pull-ups.

I recently got a message from a 21-year-old, who asked if I like to be spanked by younger men. Perfectly legitimate question. I replied that I love younger men, but I prefer to play with men who aren't young enough to be my son. He then wrote:

if I was your son, I'd start practicing incest.

Ohhhhkay. I know that was meant as a compliment, but that's a great big "ewwww" there, son.

Hi mommy,
I love to be spanked by mommy when I am a
bad boy.

Hmmm...you're 28, so I really *could* be your
mommy. Thanks for rubbing it in. Sorry, honey—for
the 27 millionth time, I don't spank. Now go away
before Mommy puts arsenic in your juice box.

I'm imagining you as my gorgeous mom and I'm
a teenager who's developing a deep sexual
attraction for you.

(shuddering) Thank you for the "gorgeous." But
otherwise—no, no, no, no, NO.

I'd love for you to play bad mommy with me
and mollest me in my sleep

Why don't you go to sleep and dream that I'm
molesting you, sonny boy. Because it won't happen
any other way.

"Nipple play"...I like a woman who loves's it,
and wants it. Would love to explore your
nipples and figure out what makes you go
crazy.

Where in any of my spanking ads were you able to
infer that I loves's nipple play? I don't; I hates's it.

i saw Your page in the LA Dommes group. i am
a sub from London and have been stroking to
Your pics for the last 2 hours. i can perform for

You on my webcam and amuse You and do ANYTHING You want me to.

This is clearly a case of mistaken identity. I don't even know who the LA Dommes are. And I ask you—is there anything, anywhere in my profile that states or even implies that I'm a Domme? (shaking head) I wanted to write to the poor fool and tell him he'd been jerkin' his gherkin for two hours over the wrong woman, but didn't have the heart.

Hello Goddess,

i hope You are well. i am a chronic wanker from ....London..... i hope to be Your cash cock and wanker and serve YOu. i can send You my bands website and stuff and You can blackmail me and make me aend regularly. i hav webcam and can do ANYTHING humiliating for You to hpotot and record, even ladies lingerie etc. i am on yahoo mess id xxxxxxxxxxxx, if You want to discuss and enslave me, i would be honoured

on my knees
wanker

Please. Shut up. You lost me at Hello.

I managed to figure out that "hpotot" was supposed to be "photo." But "make me aend"? That one has me stumped.

I am 44 years old white guy want to be your slave [phone number] sex slave Xxxx I live in Hollywood zip code xxxxx with me you can do whatever I like when I was beaten and humiliated. You can piss my mouth, you can beat my eggs can have my ass hole, I suck dick and I lick pussy

Beat his eggs?? Fine, I'll play Domme for a few minutes. Here's your order: Go write "I will not send such unsolicited filth to a woman ever again" 100 times. And I mean write, not type. With a pen. In your toes.

i have a ? if i am 15 years old anD i have a 9 inch penis hard is that big jw ?

Huh? OK, I'm a proofreader. I'm supposed to be able to decipher things. But I cannot figure out for the life of me what "jw" means. And yes, dear, nine inches is big. So are your dreams.

i love ur picturer
i got so hard

Thank you. I do try to take a good picturer.

id love 2 spank ya then shoot a huge load all over that booty while ur face down ass up looking bak at me..message me back if u want a spanking and mu cum as bad as i wanna give it 2 u

Sorry, hon. You'll have to give your computer screen its usual deposit once again—I'm not interested.

> wow you are so beautiful and berry sexy... as your boyfriend or some one.ever come back of you and eat your pusy and your ass while you are doing the splits.. that is so hot... i dont mean to say this in a bad why... do please dont take it in a bad why... is just a question... and something you might like princess

Wow, I'm berry sexy? What a grape compliment. Don't worry, I'm not going to plum the depths of lame fruit puns. Orange you glad? Anyway, if this guy didn't mean to say this in a bad why, er, way, I'd hate to see what his idea of a bad way is. Princess is not amused.

Last week, I received a friend request, and when I checked out the man's profile, it looked harmless enough. I recall that he mentioned something about how good life was, and how much he loved his wife. Awww. So I clicked Accept. Within a couple of minutes, I got this from him:

> Dam, you are one sexy lady id love to eat your ass.

Ugh. Do you kiss your loving wife with that mouth?

> wow your so hot your pics made me so hard if ok plz add me to yahoo id love to show u sometime just how hard u make me if ok that is well if so im at [deleted]@yahoo.com hugs babe

No. Not OK. Not even close. Maybe he types so badly because his keyboard is sticky.

mmmm i would love to bend u over and slowly lick down ur back and then ass till i got to ur clit and as i barried my face in ur ass an pussy i would get faster and faster till u came all over my mouth mmmm yumm hit me up

You know what's really weird? All this inappropriate crap from a total stranger, and I'm fixating on his unique spelling of "buried." Once a proofreader, always a proofreader.

After duly copying it and adding it to my ever-growing list, I deleted it. Then a few minutes later, I received:

whats up i guess u dont want to talk :(

Is he kidding? Could it be that he was truly mystified that I didn't want to respond to that charming tidbit he sent me? The mind reels.

you look amazing! wouldnt mind eating you out

You wouldn't? Really? Wow, thank you. That's good to know. Wouldn't want to inconvenience you or anything.

omg...i got so big n hard looking at the bottoms of your pretty feet...i am stroking my cock to your feet...i like kissing licking n rubbing your pretty soft sexy feet and everything else...when can we meet? your hot!

Not my thing, dude. Go to your neighborhood Payless Shoes and have yourself a party.

i would love to eat your pussy, and massage your tit's, and as soon as you dont think you can take anymore slip my dick in, and fuck you untill you cum mutiple time's, i would enjoy having you on top, and taking you from behind, and lick your pussy to tease while changing positions then shooting my load where ever you like.

Wherever I like, huh? All rightie then—Go shoot it off the top of Mt. Everest. In the snow. Naked. Don't think of it as freezing to death—think of it as being hard forever!

Sweety if I spanked you I'm afraid I would simply lose my load right in my pants.

I'm afraid if you spanked me, I'd lose my breakfast.

hey there just saw your profile and when i started to read it i got a woody.

Well, good for you. Now be careful and don't get any splinters in your hands.

I would love to have you suck my cock while I spank that ass good

No, honey, I don't think you'd like that at all. You see, when my ass is being spanked good, I have a tendency to grit my teeth.

Great ass, I see why you like to make good use of it.

Do you have a hairy brown beaver to boot?

My beaver says it's none of your dam business.

> You have a very nice-looking bottom. My only suggestion is that you spread your legs just the tiniest bit more, so that we very lucky gentlemen could also see your clitoris hanging out (as it appears to be, and a few of your marvelous pubic hairs hanging out from the front/back.

Fascinating. Thanks for sharing, and in such detail. I seem to be missing one little detail, myself—I don't recall asking you for your suggestion. There's a reason I keep my legs closed in my pictures, sweetie—I don't need people taking gynecological inventory.

Since we're in suggestion mode, I have one for you—take a refresher course in female anatomy. The clitoris doesn't "hang out." You're thinking of the labia, I believe. Shall I draw you a picture?

> baby I would take you over my knee and spank your bare ass naughty girl. I would also suck your toes and lick your pussy all night omg your so sexy.

Keep that mouth and tongue the hell away from me; I can't even begin to imagine where they've been. And again with the pussy thing. I told you, leave my cat alone. She doesn't like you.

I want to be straddled by you, which would you prefer, my face or my groin?

That's kind of like asking me if I'd prefer cottage cheese or oatmeal, Prince Charming. Both make me sick.

You sure are pretty. If I ever get the chance to spank you, would you allow me to spread open your yummy cheeks as you order me "Xxxxxxx, make out with my asshole as if you were kissing your first loves lips"

Gaaaaaaa! Definitely brings a whole new meaning to "kiss my ass."

Here's a tip, Junior. Do not liken a woman's lips to her anus. It's a very unflattering image.

Nice piece of pudding, I'd like to dig in with my tongue!

Just remember, it isn't figgy pudding.

My name Is Xxxx and I saw your profile and would like to know if you would like to have your own personal pussy eating/ass licking slave who will service your legs,pussy and ass orally in anyway that you desire.I just love sucking on pussy,licking a womans ass all over,rimming her and taking her verbal commands on how she enjoys getting pleased for as long as she desires.I can orally please you nonstop in anyway that you choose for as long as you enjoy it.I would love to be your new pussy eating/ass licking slave if you desire one.I look forward to serving you.

(groan) How do you serve someone orally when you never stop talking?

I am 6'3, 275, D/D free, non drinker, non smoker, THICK, long lasting and can cum multiple times if the feelings right

Good for you, I guess. Let me get this straight: You're just one inch taller than my boyfriend, yet you weigh about 100 pounds more than he does? I'll say you're THICK. Sorry, but I'm not into guys whose necks are bigger around than my thigh.

After being spanked your probably all wet I would be able to tell by the aroma that I love so well. Then I would like to lick you taste you ah the smell and taste of a woman. Mmmmm

Ah, the sound of an idiot. Do we taste like chicken?

I will spank you into submission. You are hot your Master knows that. I just would like to become worthy of being in your circle. Very respectful single clean shaved 8" available anytime for you.

You want to be worthy? You can start by not announcing the length of your shlong to a perfect stranger.

I want to take you from behind, that's my favorite especially I want to dominate you from behind, with my large hands wrap around your throat. The variety of what can be done from behind is so great; it can open up new pleasure centers and different angles of penetration. I like it all, standing up while our hips grind together, fully embraced with my hands cupping your breasts and pinching your nipples. I want to grab your ass checks sticking it straight in the air so I can penetrate you from a steep angle like a jackhammer, flexing my knees and thighs every time I thrust all the way deep into you're wetness. I than want you just lying down, on your stomach, legs spread wide and continue to enter slowly and deeply from behind then wrap my warm (hot) body around yours, biting and kissing the back of your neck, whispering dirty thoughts into your ear again and again, tightly embracing your arms so our bodies are one, watching your face change between the smile and tensions of ultimate pleasure every time I slide in and out of you.

There were several more paragraphs of this blather, but I chose to spare you. This gives you the general idea.

A few random thoughts:
1. Ass checks? My ass doesn't have checks. I prefer polka dots.
2. If I wanted to have sex with a jackhammer, I'd buy one at Home Depot.

3. Are you warm, or are you hot? Make up your damn mind.

4. If I'm lying face-down on the bed, how can you watch my face change?

5. You just want our bodies to be one so you can share my brain, as yours is clearly deficient.

Received this right before the world was supposed to end, according to the Mayan calendar:

> I have admit seeing you and your lovely red bare bottom being spanked caused a little rise
> :)

Emphasis on "little," I'm sure. Really? You just had [to] admit this? Your last act on this earth before the Rapture? Looks like you didn't have much of a life to begin with.

Courtesy of a 19-year-old (!!):

> im xxxxxx, i was checking out ur pics and i love ur ass ;] id love to lick it and fucking it ;]

My, my. Don't let your mommy catch you using naughty words like that, little boy.

> bare bottom ass whippings with my belt that will make u squirt your cum across the room and u wont be able to sit down for a week

The only thing that's going to squirt across the room is my projectile vomit. Go away.

> Would love to spank you and then mount you with my large hard cock.....sexy rich guy looking for some kinky fun

I saw your picture, Richie Rich. You're lying about the sexy part, so you're probably lying about the large cock too.

> Im pretty new to this site & came across ur photo. Im a tattoo artist fro. San diego. Im very much into the tits & bottoms of a lady. Being a tattoo artist i do enjoy inflicking some pain into my sex, spanking, tit squeezing, anal sex on a women & some biting. I do like to take control when were having sex.. BUT I ALSO LIKE BEING BIT & SCRATCHED HARD ENOUGH TO DRAW BLOOD...

Tattoo artist, huh? Since you enjoy inflicking [sic] pain and you like a bit of pain yourself, here's a tat suggestion. Tattoo "I'm with" on one testicle and "Stupid" on the other. And on your cock? That's right: "Stupid." That is, assuming it's big enough to accommodate six letters.

This gem is from a man with a nice close-up shot of his erect member:

> surrender your mind and body then fuck luke rabbits. Let's talk and make it happened.

I don't know who Luke is, but I don't want to fuck him or his rabbits.

I wish I had a room with cages, chains, whips and other toys for you...desire to have you tied up with ropes

give you spank, whip, hear moaning, suck and bite your breasts, bite your buttocks, penetrate your vagina and your anus all night

fornicate in the streets, in the forest, in the car... but also want a wife, a girlfriend, a friend, a lover

You want four women? How greedy of you.

For the last 18 months, I have been "involved" with a lovely, stacked redhead who just cannot get enough spanking ... seeps as if the harder I spank her, the hotter she gets ... we work on squirting as well, and during our last "session" she got so hot being spanked that she soaked the bed with her ejaculation ... which was HOT.

If you are interested in an encounter with a mature couple ... participating in hard spanking threesome fun, let me know and we can set up a "spanking conference" to introduce ourselves.

(scrubbing vigorously with brain bleach) Ummm, no. No, thank you. And speaking of bleach, you may want to do some laundry.

I would love to spank you hard. And afterwards, go down on you, have insane sex with you and

102

again spank you when you need to get wet... I am sub but also love to spank and play with a woman like you... I bet you get so wet...

I'm quite wet now, honey. Know why? Because reading this crap brought on a powerful need to take a shower.

And finally: Apparently, this gentleman felt I needed a masturbation manual:

I want to confess that I had a fantasy thinking about you..I was thinking how nice it would be if i could ask you to do things and you would do them..And you could ask me as well..I was thinking of asking you to place your left hand on your labia, pulled up slightly and allow your clitoris to pop between your fingers on your left hand.. Then take your index finger, lick it softly, then rub ever so softly on your clitoris, making slow circles..I am dying to know how long you could do until you couldn't stand it any more..Sounds like fun to me.

You know, you could have consolidated all that gibberish into one sentence: "I want to watch you masturbate." I applaud your flowery efforts, but the answer is still no.

Have I scarred you for life yet? Are you wishing you could unread this chapter? If not, wait. I still have more.

For those who are thinking by now that crass cluelessness is purely a man's territory, read on.

Yup, Girls Too

Unfortunately, this book does tend to show men in a bad light. But yes, I do get these gems from women on occasion as well. Not many, to be sure. Perhaps if I were into F/F, I'd hear from more women who want to play with me. This chapter will be short, but entertaining nonetheless.

> how about a little i spank you you spank me
> over the telephone
> write immediately

First of all, honey, sorry, I don't play with girls. Second, I don't top. Third, I don't do phone-spank. And fourth—write immediately? I don't take orders either, Mistress.

> one hot milf.id love to have some nude pics
> sweeteeeee.send to xxxxxxxxx@xxxxxxx.com
> and ill send some your way baby

Sorry, sweeteeeee, I'm not into illiterate women any more than I am into illiterate men.

> You have the most beautiful eyes. If you ever want to have fun with a girl and her German Shepherd, let me know.

Please tell me she's talking about a man from Stuttgart who tends sheep...

Hello, how are you doing? I like the outfits and shoes you are wearing in the last pic on the first row of your photo gallery, the 1st and 3rd pics on the first row of the 2nd page of the gallery, the first and last pics on the 2nd row of the 2nd page, the last 2 pics on the 3rd row of the 2nd page, the 3rd pic on the 5th row of the 2nd page, the last 3 pics on the 2nd row of the 3rd page, and the pic on the last row of the 3rd page, can you send all those outfits to me?

I can't even begin to follow this. Perhaps I should send you ALL my clothes and be done with it.

This one isn't crass, but it pissed me off. I received it on Alt.com, from a fem-domme. I guess she skipped over the part in my profile where I said that I only play with men. Actually, I think she skipped my profile altogether.

In town for biz. ARe you available for use?

How does this offend me? Let me count the ways.

First, what kind of introduction is that? I understand the need to be dominant, but come on; have some manners, for God's sake. Second, what makes her think she can just breeze into town and pick up on a perfect stranger for immediate gratification? What incredible nerve. Third—for use? Screw you, lady. I'm not a piece of equipment. And fourth, if she had bothered to read my profile, she would have seen that I am a spanko, not a sub (my headline on Alt blatantly reads: NOT a sub, just a bottom!), and that she was wasting her time and mine by writing to me at all. John said that in the BDSM world, this bit of correspondence would be perfectly appropriate. Whatever. It's not appropriate in my world.

> Hows it goin??? Ur hot I wanna c u naked and riding a dick.

Really? I want a lot of things. At the moment, I wanna c u go away.

> HELLO U SEXI BIATCH

Want to know I think? (That was rhetorical; I'm going to tell you anyway.) I think that whoever started that whole biatch/beeyotch thing should be shot. Seriously.

> It is amazing that someone your age has such a wonderful bottom

(sigh) Yes, it's amazing. I'm a freak of nature.

> Hi Erica , my name is [deleted] I just wanted to say I was asked to be spanked across my ample bottom ... I am so naughty lately and justly deserve it but an so embarrassed to be bare bottomed and humiliated ... Any suggestions I know I can't hold out they are ready to doank any moment and I do not have a choice.. My bottom is swelling with anticipation . So are breasts he plans to tug and pull them a bit I imagine.. Here we Go....

What am I supposed to say to this, really? Thanks for sharing? Happy doanking? (What is doanking?)

Oh, and her bottom is swelling with anticipation? Hmmm. Sounds to me like an excuse why she can't get her jeans on.

hmmm - - Jewish bare bottoms look just like Catholic bare bottoms
interesting

WTF??

What did you expect? A little yarmulke on each butt cheek? Bruises in the shape of the Star of David? What kind of mind even conceives of this sort of comparison? It's truly disturbing. I think we should recite an *Ave Maria* for this woman. Or, in my case, an *Oy Vey Maria*. (Yes, I'm going to hell. We established that a long time ago.)

Saving the best for last. Brace yourself; this one is long, and it's extremely graphic. Aside from removing the names, I have not changed a word:

Hi - I'm Xxxxx and my husband is Xxxx.

I told Xxxx about my being bi-curious and seeking to explore my desire to be with another woman a few months ago, to which he was very supportive. Also Xxxx and I are curious about trying a 3-some. I am a 5-8 , 34B-28-34 redhead (my titties as Xxxx likes me to call them are small yet my nipples are super sensitive, I can cum from having them sucked on which I really enjoy as does Xxxx sucking them). Xxxx is 5-8 with hazel eyes and an 8 inch cock.

We're interested in our special friendship to hopefully include even spending vacation time together with you. Lets explore our sensuality together as we become special intimate friends and lovers.

We both enjoyed looking at your photo.as it gave us the idea of you possibly role playing with us. We're interested in role playing options such as teacher and school girl, boss and secretary interviewing new applicant, chambermaid and hotel guests or any role play you'd like to try - though either Sexy Sister with her Sister and her Husband gets us excited with sexy sisters making love with each other or putting on a show for Xxxx, to even my sexy sister seducing my husband Xxxx as I then join in for a fun love fest, as does a Mommy-Daddy role with you as our sexy daughter which is our favorite and possibly most exciting for us, such as being Xxxx's daddy's little girl which excites him, along with my mommy's little girl too as this really makes us hot for you. maybe with our naughty daughter licking mommy's pussy or suck daddy's cock s before dinner or bed or taking showers together -.from there - who knows what will follow ?

Please don't be offended, but I believe it best to be open and honest about what we're looking for.

Xxxx would like for us to become friends sharing sexy erotic emails with revealing hot photos and a many heated phone calls, then soon afterwards hopefully meet in person at a public location such as a Starbucks for a latte. We can let our friendship then develop to hopefully also allow us to make our fantasy desires a reality, or just stay friends if you want.

Lets start things off by sharing regular emails about our personal likes-dislikes and daily lives, along with also including sexy hot details about our inner desires or fantasies that hopefully we can make 'cum' true for each other one day soon, along with sharing revealing sexual photos. We can tell each other our special desires for the other or both of us at once for you - you can share your desires for me - Xxxx or both of us.

I am curious to experience the joy Xxxx gets when playing with my breasts, by fondling and sucking your breasts, hoping it makes you cum as it does make me climax when Xxxx sucks mine. My nipples are very sensitive and I get very wet when he sucks my nipples as I would like you' to let me suck your nipples and you to suck my nipples for starters.

I am also curious to watch you with Xxxx, you sucking his cock or Xxxx sucking your breasts, plus his filling your wet pussy or if you'd like filling your tight butt with his cock as I then join in, sucking your nipples-feeding you mine to suck or licking Xxxx's cock as it slides in-out of your pussy as I also lick your pussy at the same time - or what ever gets me wet as we're both very oral in our love making From here we can enjoy each other as a pair or a 3-some in any combination possible - with all involved open to the experience - seeking joy and pleasure.

Hugs plus more - Xxxxx (mommy if this excites you too)

PS- we travel often over holiday weekends and the summer several times on vacation so meeting can be easily arranged and we can be discreet if need be. We can also host you as our guest when we have you visit us at our expense. If you want, we can just remain intimate pen pals sharing hot emails along with heated phone calls and friends for the time being, with the option for more intimate personal times in the future when you're ready. Due to our jobs we are not comfortable posting photos here, though we will send them to your regular email if ok with you - we can exchange photos together.

Has your brain blown to smithereens yet? Mine did, about 2/3 of the way through. What possesses people to introduce themselves in this manner? Do others actually reply to this crap? Is this just another type of form letter that this woman tosses out far and wide and hopes someone will answer? I'd like to think it isn't real, that it's just a sick joke. But I'm afraid it isn't. There are too many details; I'm thinking it's quite real.

Roleplay with me as their daughter?? I'm older than they are!

I don't want you to play with my breasts. I don't want anyone to play with my breasts. I'm a spanko. The area of needed attention is farther south.

I don't want a "3-some" with a gruesome twosome. And I'm not interested in your 5' 8" husband. My boyfriend is 6' 2", thank you very much.

First you're my Sexy Sister, then you're my Mommy. My sister, my mother, my sister, my mother...SLAP! Make up your mind.

Now that I've thoroughly shamed both genders, what's next? How about an extra dose of arrogance?

FULL OF YOURSELF, MUCH?

It's already been well established that I identify as a bottom, not as a submissive. I don't have a problem with D/s, truly I don't. But since it's not my thing, I don't like it when people assume that it is. Especially when some Joe Schmo in cyberspace barks an order at me and thinks that's going to be effective. If I *were* submissive, it would be to a top who has taken the time and care to earn my trust and respect; a man in whose hands I feel safe. The following clowns need not apply.

> I thinks it' time someone out tht nauaghty little bottem,over there for a long haed spanking! And I' the one to do to! i will excpect a response from you abou 15 min is taht under stood!

You thinks, Popeye? Perhaps you'd better thinks again. Here's a hint, people. This kind of correspondence *can* be hot—if you actually know the person. And if you take a few extra seconds and don't make over a dozen ridiculous typos in three sentences.

> bend over u nawtie gurl....pull ur pants down and show me your panties.....NOW

I have a better idea. You bend over backward and disappear up your own ass...NOW.

> Yous bitch will want ta take ma cock in ya mout and suk on it, cos yous my bitch

Yous got to be kidding.

> I am going to spank your ass then horse fuck you pain will happen but you will beg for more

Wanna bet? Interesting qualifier—pray tell, how does horse fucking differentiate from any other fucking? On second thought, you know what? I don't want to know. I'm not a horse. Go away.

> am sure that you need a dark red colour on your ass if i spank you you will screaming all the time do me add

Yeah, screaming, "Get away from me!" And no, I did not him add.

> you are stupid girl, and i will take your booty my knee and give you good spank, will you have that? =)

Not as stupid as you are if you think I'm letting you anywhere near my booty. No, I will not have that.

> I want you to submitt yourself to my world of fantasy situations where your deepest desires can be fullfilled. Write to me here and I will develope a story line just for you kitten. You will serve me and my harem in a realm like no other ever known.

First, in my fantasy world, tops know how to spell *submit* and *fulfilled*. Second, I ain't your kitten, or any other kind of pet. Nor am I your genie...harem?? Third, before you develope [sic] a storyline, you might want to develop some writing skills.

> Get in the tub with some cold water and then give me a call for some phone sex your pics have me rockhard

So many answers come to mind. Here are just a few:
1. Seems to me that I'm not the one who needs a tub of cold water.
2. Oh, I'd love to, but you forgot to give me your phone number, asshat.
3. This is the paramedic. Erica was in such a rush to obey your orders, she slipped and knocked herself unconscious on the bathtub rim.

> I have been a Master/Daddy for 25 years. The perfect little girl never questions her Master/Daddy, and thinks of his needs above her own.

Damn shame I'm not perfect, huh? This little girl's need, at the moment, is for you to take your ginormous Dom ego and...well, you figure it out.

Here's a twist. This landed in my mailbox on Alt last week; a top writing with the express purpose of telling me off.

> Wow. Your profile has been up and repulsivd for so long, I must respond. I'm a Dom. I don't need you. I teach and find hour disinterest in my work an insult. You "advertise" relentlessly.

114

I find your consistancy and repetitve requests annoying. Things must just be going great for you since you're still here. I can meet your need and send you off, but damn, you need to expand ylur interests. Respond if interested.

So, I guess you won't be joining the Erica Scott Fan Club anytime soon? Too bad, so sad.

I had questions, of course. My disinterest in his work? I don't know this guy; how would I have disinterest in his work? So I checked out his profile. As one would expect, he's heavy into D/s and protocol, and claims to specialize in "teaching and training subs and fledglings" and helping them fully realize their desire to serve. Ah, now I get it. In my profile, I stress that I am a bottom, not a sub, and while I love confident and toppy men, I have no interest in masters, daddies, teachers, or trainers. The poor dear egomaniac took that personally, it seems.

And after that mini-tirade, he tells me to respond if interested? Right. Because I'm that masochistic; I want to play with someone who thinks I'm repulsive and annoying.

John suggested that I write back to him, being unfailingly polite, which would completely bamboozle him. I agree that could be fun, but it's just not my style. I did absolutely nothing; I didn't respond at all. I figured that would piss him off the most.

However, in the interest of fantasy, here's what I would have replied to him:

"Dear Almighty Dom Fathead,

Yup, I'm still here. I met my current play partner, and my last partner before him, on here. So yes, things really are going great for me, thanks.

I guess things are going equally great for you, since you took the time in your busy training schedule to write to someone you find so repulsive.

Expand my interests? To what, may I ask? Being a human doormat? Nah. My interests are just fine as they are. I figure if they annoy the likes of you, I must be on the right track.

Honey, you couldn't meet my need on your best day. You wouldn't have any idea how to deal with a woman with a brain and a voice. Go back to your fledglings and rule your pathetic little roost, your mindless masses. And really, if you find my profile so offensive, please stop viewing it. I know you have better things to do."

And finally, here's someone who didn't care for my profile's request for a well-written email.

What kind of bottom/sub are you - demanding a "well written e-mail." You're gonna judge my writing? HA!!!!

State whether you take a heavy spanking; whether I can fuck your red ass afterward; your donation; and don't give me any more lectures about no fancy e-mailin.

Interesting. I had no idea that asking for a well-written message was "lecturing." In my imagination, he received this response:

"Dear Sir: What kind of bottom am I? A smart one who appreciates intelligent tops. Let's see: Yes, I take a heavy spanking. No, you can't do anything to my ass except spank it, not that I'd let you do that, either. Donation? Why don't you donate your brain to science, so that perhaps they can figure out where things went awry and rectify that for future generations? Thanks for your interest. Oh, and please go fuck yourself."

Had enough of the outrageously inflated egos? Next, we'll go from the arrogant to the illegible (well, even more illegible than it's been, so far).

TYPING WHILE WANKING

Most of the entries in this book are badly written. However, there are some that are so completely screwed up in every way, you figure the writer had to be typing with one hand. Because no one could be this illiterate. Right? Please say yes.

> if u like wt u see n want me to rock ur world in style, then email me ur. n lets have the best ever,.talk to u soon

(groan) What can I say about this? It gives me a headache just to read it. And is anyone besides me sick to death of the expression "rock your world"?

> hope youare good I miss have a souil grilfeiend a lot cant you make some more hose feet pic show me your feet in hose love big xxxxx p.s have you have a boy friend yet

Huh?? OK, I do get the part that he wants to see pictures of my feet. Not going to happen. But what's a souil grilfeiend?

Same guy, I think:

> hope evey is good with you I love to see some more hose pic and some your feet in the pic four me some some love ok right back big xxxxx

You want to see hose pics? Might I suggest you visit an online garden store?

> yo wats up sexxi..u got yahoomessenger?if u want 2 see my cock on my web cam ..and ill do w/e u want me 2 do on cam ..wats ur sn 4 yahoomessenger?

Yeah, yeah, Im 2 sexxi. Sorry, I don't have Yahoo Messenger. But my AOL screen name is InYourDreamsMoron.

So I finally gave in and got Yahoo Messenger:

> hey sexy how u doin, like ....ur.... energy n wanted 2 show swome love, u gotta aim or yahoo mssnger?

Yes, I do have Yahoo IM. Here's the address: nochanceinhell4u. (I ended up deleting the program.)

> heyyy Erica (sexy) can we b friends i was cumming 2 california soon and wanted 2 know if i cod cum by and giv ur ass a lil spanking if u and ur bf wodnt mind

Cod? Sounds fishy to me. And yes, I wod mind very much.

> u horny like cam to cam wow i can tell u hide nice boobs there wonder what size tehy r look hot

All that wanking must have affected your eyesight, dear, if you think my boobs are my best asset.

> damn ur hot
> nice pic and pro

119

> where u stay at
> and u got messenger ??
> very nice ass hun ;)

Where I stay at? Somewhere very, very far from u, hun.

> wow sexy woman you like cyber sex with know webcam to webcam sex tel me fast sexy i love you

No, I like real sex. And not with you.

> im new to the seen how did u start what got u into it when was ure first spanking how was it who was it

This is fascinating. Five questions in one sentence, and not one capital letter or punctuation mark. New to the seen [sic]? I do believe he's new to writing, too.

> ello ow are you. Am loking where to get the best spanking pics of you or others i have a lot but i have a passion for that and also videos of aunt jennifer,s tanks do you have a place to recomend mee

Why, yes, I do. Look up your local chapter of Illiterates Anonymous. We admitted we were powerless over participles, and our writing had become unreadable.

wow i am the man you are looking for and more hi i am xxx i am 30 and i am 5'10 and i am dd free and my cock is 7 and 3 wd and i fun and i love sex and i can do it any time and any where and and more

Easy, boy. Just back away from the Red Bull. That's one hell of a run-on sentence you've got going there. Hey, how can your cock be 7 when you're 30? Did you not have a cock for your first 23 years?

hi u nauthgy young lady i am a pro . spanker n more in store u have a butt beauifull n it lokkks like it needs one of mine over the knee enjoying straring out style spanking -paddling/ croping n to top it off my cat of -12- tails- i travl for all over for work -wwe manger- i also did make 3 movies tne best one is the taletail a delitfull spankings of all the ways n more i am 51 a lifestyler d/d free -w/male - live in flornce 5 min. from airport n going to calf. late july love to take u out for dinner n sees how u enjoy my style butt u have a beauifull butt n boby

There's no way I could make this up. I couldn't conceive of this degree of illiteracy. Amazingly, he did spell *spanker* and *spanking* correctly.

Well, despite this delitfull [sic] missive, I think I will turn down the dinner offer. The thought of his "more in store" makes me throw up in my mouth a little.

Hi, I know what u mean,not a sub you think like I do.you r a bottom--great one also---I have

50yrs.in the scene. I know what u want, I was in LEATHER ROSE Chi. many yrs. ago--know just how to please a Bottom, like u....I love your honesty! put the bozos in their place, My b day is Mar.17th. St. PADDLE. me day,ha ha,Id give u u my spanks,mmmmmm now back to u young lady,If i had u otk, i would take u (flying)---term 4 when you get soooo excited u get dizzy and shake as u orgasm.--not being crude just hot-wet moist. My uncle "tanned"my 16yr.old cousin 2-3x a week,that started my SPANKING career. got a chubby and loved to spank since then. You must have gotten hot when some one paddled u otk how old were u, first spanking???tets chat---lost my lil bottom 4yrs ago. play safe ---lets talk...a friend??I lived in Yuca Valley yrs ago take care

My dear fellow, I had many reactions to this, but "hot-wet moist" wasn't one of them. Put the bozos in their place, huh? Will do. **plunk**

hello sexy Erica nice pucture i lovit welcom take pictures on horse

Why on earth would I take a pucture, er, picture on a horse? Who am I, a kinky Dale Evans? (happy taaaiiils, to you)

hay there iam a lil unrr age but i wont tell if you won't

Hay? Again with the horse references? And yes, he was definitely unrr age—17.

122

You know, even when I put that through my English to Moron dictionary, I couldn't figure out what he was trying to say. Any guesses?

We've come to the point where I have plenty of entries left over, but they don't fit into any particular category. Best for last, maybe? ("Best" being written with tongue firmly planted in cheek.)

I'll take "Jackass Potpourri" for $1000, Alex.

MISCELLANEOUS MAYHEM

This chapter will be a little of everything, I think. These gems might have fit into other chapter themes—some are brief, some are long-winded, most are inarticulate, all are inappropriate. But I think I also have some unusual ones as well. You can judge for yourself.

First up: A whole bunch you can file under "Please read my profile, dumbass." You know, the place where I take extra special care to specify what I'm seeking so there won't be any misunderstanding? Spanking, not sex. I don't switch. And so on. Perhaps someday, someone will explain to me why this is so incomprehensible.

> iam very much into spanking giving getting and watching and you are very pertie and i wouldnt my being spanked by you well looking for friend who into spanking to

I really need to update my profile and highlight on it in several places, "I DON'T SPANK!" But thanks for saying I'm pertie.

> what is your hand like like?do u get to the point when u spank someone erica?when will u put me otk the spanking.need prove that u r capable of getting to the point of things.its time for spanking.does that hand of your need some work give it.

What part of "I'm a bottom" do you not comprehend? I ask you once again, people—is there anything, anywhere within my page, that indicates I do the spanking? Granted, if I did have any latent topping tendencies in me, they would be brought to the fore by idiotic comments like this.

May I pay your bills and be your slave?

Honey, I have no use for slaves. For the millionth time, I'm a bottom. But hey, if you have piles of extra money strewn about and you want to cough up a check for my rent and my exorbitant health insurance premiums, be my guest.

Hello Nudist Lady:

I am a single and sensual Scorpio man who would love to meet you and share sensual good times...

I am a nudist who enjoys going to nude beaches and nudist resorts and looking for a lady to join him...

Have you ever been naked in public...

WTF? Where did he get that I'm a nudist? Have I been naked in public...hmmm. Would a spanking/pool/Jacuzzi party count? If so, then yes.

hey will u trade naked pics with me?? i'll send u some of me or my sexy bi gf if ur into that. what do u say??

What do I say? I say, is your screen so covered with your Jackson Pollock spatterings that you can't read my profile?

> If we got together after some friendly email exchange which one(s) of the items below would bring you the most pleasure
> 1. a good spanking
> 2. a "kiss it and make it well" soothing session after the spanking
> 3. soothing my tender spanking hand with those thick warm juices flowing between your legs
> 4. smothering me in your feminity between those big dds
> 5. an hour long foreplay
> 6. allowing me to slip a key body part deep inside you
> 7. giving this bad boy a good spanking

Damn, he was doing so well with 1. and 2., and then went spectacularly downhill. And...my big what?? Dearest, you clearly have me confused with someone else. DD, indeed. I couldn't smother a field mouse.

This one was from a 19-year-old:

> I think you are super hot. Can we fuck?

Well, I know I can, and I suppose you can too. Oh, you mean with each other? Not a chance.

This was from a man wearing a Day-Glo purple wig:

how about foot TICKLING???
or role playing ???
I am nearby in SFV
like translesbians in thigh boots like me ???
call me

If I liked foot TICKLING, I would have said so in my PROFILE.

wow sexy and u have sexy feet i like to lick and kiss your feet

That's nice. Go find someone who would enjoy that.

And finally:

am ready to be all yours, your bitch boy, your sissy maid , your whore and more,

am ready to worship you at your feet, ask you for mercy while am licking your shoes, i`ll be your pet and i`ll live in a cage if u want me to

amd ready to be owned, humiliated, am ready to follow your commands and be punished dor not to,

please make me your loyal slave Mistress

(sigh) I am not a Domme. I am not a Domme. I am not a Domme. Have I made that perfectly clear? Apparently not. You want commands? OK. Find a Domme and leave me alone.

Ideally, a proper spanking, great message of the red ass, and them I desire to give oral pleasure. Feel I am an expert at Gspot stimulation.

What I want to know is, how does a red ass intercept a message? Don't answer that. Gspot stimulation—if the G stands for Gag, then it's working.

hey sexy, hows it going? damn, i like youre little naughty side! that ass is killer babe. let me slap that ass baby!

(sigh). I suppose I could mention the fact that an "ass" is a farm animal until I turn blue in the face, but it simply won't take with some people. And why, why, WHY is it so hard for people to get the difference between "your" and "you're"? *Your* is the possessive of you. *You're* is a contraction of you are. Got it? Yeah, I'm testy. This isn't rocket science, folks.

i would love to spank that ass erica
thats a hot ass you have lady

Again with the ass. And now that you mention it, my ass is *not* hot at the moment, it's rather cold. I do hope to remedy that soon. But not with you.

how r u beautiful ??? MMMMay I say Erica, awwwwwwwwwhata hotttie u r babeee :-) Ur simply stunnnnnnnnnin' darlin' *grins* I loveeeeeee ur profile & pix (Especially,the one where ur on the bed & the captian reads something like " I bet u'd love 2 get ur hands on

this" HELLLL YEAHHHHHHHHH !!! *S* ......But I
am wondering,(hope u dont think it strange) if
u wear flipflops at all ??? AND if so, do u ever
get spanked with them ??? ....I use to do this
2 a woman I use 2 be with :-) ...... and what
other objects might be used in ur spankin'
rituals ? mwaaah

You know what? I don't even know where to begin
with this one, so I think I'll let it stand on its own
splendor and you guys can come up with your own
comments. But just for the record? No, I don't wear
flip-flops. And if I did, they would stay on my feet,
thank you. I have a strong objection to being
spanked with footwear.

I'm lloking for a sub who I can develop my skill
with. you seem very direct abou twaht you
want and I would like to make use of you and
your knowledge. I want to spank you and she
what that's like.

HEY! Leave my *twaht* out of this.

I'm not a sub. Nor am I a hoagie, or a hero, or
any other kind of sandwich. You want to make use
of me? What am I, an iPod? Finally, I'm not a
guinea pig. I don't offer up my bottom for spanking
so you can "she" what it's like.

Along the same theme:

hey whats goin on! Ive really never tried full out
spanking and would love to try it out hit me up
if ur up for it

I'm sorry…did someone drug me and then tattoo "Guinea Pig" on my butt while I was unconscious?

I didn't reply, of course. Then I got this, same guy:

> hey a lot of people wont respond cause i dont have a pic! i hope u do cause im not looking for the sex so much as im lookin for my first time really spanking some one! i dont have a pic cause i get on here on my phone and cant upload off my phone! i hope u hit me up soon

FYI—no one cares about your pic. They're not responding because you're an idiot. Learn how to use apostrophes, for God's sake.

> I am looking for someone to lick… that is what I enjoy. In town for just a few days. Not sumbissive, just know what I want. Let me know if we can take care of this.

Take care of this?? He makes it sound like it's a case of jock itch. How romantic. But I'm glad to hear he's not sumbissive [sic]. In town for a few days, huh? "What'd you do on your vacation, Joe?" "Oh, I licked a few locals…"

> oooooooh…..every time I saw here you drive's me GRAZY…..

What is "grazy"? Do I give you the urge to munch on grass?

This same person, a couple of days before, also wrote me:

you are a VOLKANO.....

I'm going to assume that he meant volCano. But does he mean that I'm hot, or that I spew a lot of hot air?

The next two seem to have some sort of obsession with cooking:

> hi baby you are very sexy and very nice m very like your ass plase you like my cook if you want it plase you give your hotmail. ok kiss you now m wait for now

You know, when I first read "you like my cook," I thought, "Hot damn! He wants to make dinner for me!" Then I realized he misspelled the word, and he meant something else altogether. No, I'd rather not dine on that, thank you very much.

> my cook are so big, you have so sweet ass, i will take your booty my kne and give you really good spank, your freind here, i'm nice guy.

You know, I hear these cooks eat way too much of their own cooking—maybe that's why they're so big.

Warning: Beverage spew alert with this one!

> I've seen a lot of women really get off on having their gentiles spanked.

I may be going out on a limb here, but I do believe he meant "genitals."

I guess you could call John my Gentile; he's Catholic. But no, I don't get off having him spanked.

We live too fare apart so , , , oh well. I too am into the spanking sceen abd I just love to pink up a nice hinny.

There are times when Internet distance is a blessing to my hinny. Interesting use of commas as leader dots; haven't seen that before.

hi sexxy how are you? i would luv tog give u a good spanking..what you wearing sexxy?

What am I wearing? Take your pick: a. A frown; b. Idiot-proof underwear; or c. None of your freaking business.

nice photos you are a very sexy lady looking very hot and sexy in the low cut tops and panties also very hot body

Thank you very much. That was very nice of you, and I appreciate it very very much. Very. Have a very nice day.

im looking a spanking button i saw your profile and i understand what you want im cool with that

It took me a while, but I finally figured out he meant spanking bottom. But what a cool idea—a spanking button! What would that do—you just press it, and POOF! a spanker (or spankee) appears, exactly to your specifications? I like that even more than the "Easy" button from Staples!

I could quite easily see myself spending a few hours perfecting my forehand and reddening the cheeks of your arse. Will you allow me the pleasure? I would bring the wife along to deal with the sexual side of things as I do get horny from handing out a spanking.

Perfecting his forehand? I'm a golf ball now? And how about that last part—he hauls along "the wife" so he'll have her as a spooge receptacle after he's done working himself up spanking me? How charming. What's she supposed to do while he's busy with me, sit off to the side and go "ooh"? And more important, what am I supposed to do once he turns his attentions to her? Eww. No, thank you.

hello sexy, how are you, i am xxxx and i would love to be your new friend. an I must say damn you have a very hot an sexy ass, can i spank an kiss it.

No, you can't. Why? Well, besides the other obvious reasons, you misspelled the simple word "and" three times. I'm sorry, but that's really not a good sign.

hi u and i have the same birthday and i like to one day play with u just spanking and never want or need sex so lets start talking and getting to know each other ok ?

No. Happy birthday. Now go blow your…candles.

This one's from an 18-year-old:

MMMMM....yummy? are u interested in yound cock? id love to play. i have lots of dirty pics. please message me back. i want you.

Yes, I'm sure you do, dear. Yound? What's that? Round yound virgin? No, that's yon. Never mind.

hey there male here from california usa who spanks females otk for discplien would to take u otk for thsi im 33

I'm so glad he clarified "California, USA." I might have thought he meant California, Antarctica.

mmmmmmmmmmmmmm hunnie i wana spank that nice lil ass i love your legs u r sexy as hell

Mmmmmmmmmmmmmmm...thanks, but no thanks, hunnie.

wow hi i am [deleted] in [deleted] and 5'10 and i am very loving and caring and fun and out going and i love to pleas and kiss and i can go all day and all nit

All nit??? How very lice for you.

Hey, whats up? My name is xxxxx and yours? Anyhow, I was bored so I decided to go online. I am looking to hangout sometime maybe have some drinks, party together. Do you drink/smoke? Can you hangout tonight?

The first thing I thought was, this is a kid, maybe about 15. But no. He's 25. Hey, in another 25 years, he could be president. [yes, this too was written during the Bush administration.]

> Hi I like to spank your bottom for you,since you say that you enjoy that so thats why i like to spank your bottom hun well can we have fun with each other? i like your looks and all and you seem to be a kewl lady with a good attitude to go with it thats good Im sure you will be alright in life take care Hun

Well, at least this one said "bottom." Very kewl of him.

> You have beautiful hair, are you wearing a wig?

Now that's a new one! Trust me, this mop is mine. If you could see it before the volumizing product and the blow dryer, you wouldn't think it's a wig.

> hi...well i read your about me and your who id like to meet and well im over 18 im actually 21 lol i think your really hot i gotta admit that, hope my mail wont get ignore:)

No, dear. Your mail won't get ignore[d]. Your mail will get feature[d] on the CHoS.

> I know how to make those pretty buns nice and Red. Do i get to taste the kitty after i complete your desire?

I know this may be a foreign concept to you, but there are some men out there for whom spanking me is their desire as well, and they don't feel the need for some sort of extracurricular reward afterward. Taste the kitty, indeed.

And can someone explain to me why he capitalized Red, but he can't capitalize i?

> hi my beautiful princess my name is xxxxxx you are a very beautiful and sweet sexy girl you have a charm that you make me go crazy to me the girls as they do you me to go crazy I would like to know you and for this I hope you accept my invitation for a chat this it is my contact messenger [deleted]
>
> I kiss you
>
> compliments you have a beautiful bottom to bite and to kiss so many kisses
>
> mmmmmm you are really a stupendous and beautiful girl you are fascinating girl sweet and very beautiful mmmmmmmmche that you are

Let's start with the fact that there is no punctuation whatsoever in this mess. Next, language awkwardness notwithstanding, it makes no sense. I guess I shouldn't complain, though—I mean, he called me beautiful five times.

But what the hell is mmmmmmmmche?

> Hi Erika – I would like to be friends and get to know your bottom a bit better.

Not the rest of me? My spleen is highly insulted.

> I am proud to write nice person and happy to ask a beautiful person like u to be my friend and i am new here and i just viewed ur profile and looks soo wow and i decided to write to u and take u as my friend and i am christian whom i love the lord very much and i am soo much joy to write to u today,and i hope u will write to me and i love to know more about u.bye and hoping to hear from u .

You poor dear. Don't you know that your lord will cast you into hell for communicating with a heathen like me? Now be a good boy and go fetch your prayer book. Wash those hands first.

If I didn't think I was going to hell before, I sure do now:

> wat a desperate look all of u sinful funky its shall all fall one day for u all are plagues of moral distruction

(laughing) Ah, yes, I am a plague. Every time I open my mouth, locusts fly out. My dear, if you think my li'l old spanking fetish is the cause of moral distruction [sic], you need to get off your knees and get out more. And your first stop should be night school to take Remedial English.

> What a cutie you are! Will you please answer something for me? Please tell the truth...If you could have your could pick the ideal size for you partners erect penis to be... would you

choose... A) 5-6 inches B) 6-7 inches C) 7-8 inches D) 8-9 inches Or E) OVer 9 inches. Please have the guts to answer and be brutally honest about it. Thank alot.

You've got to be kidding me. Brutally honest, huh? All rightie...F) None of your business, numb-nuts.

Oh, and since someone or another is bound to ask—I don't have a size preference. I don't exactly bring a tape measure to bed with me. As long as it's big enough so that I don't have to ask, "Is it in yet?", I'm good.

> id like to know you more,id be your man?age is just a number i date women older than me.your hot and id appreciate a cali girl.i tan good in the summer.wanta call me.

Yes, age is just a number. So is IQ. In your case, it's a two-digit number.

> look real hot in your pics i know you have a man but if you ever break up with him i am available i read your file and i like what i z.

i z stupid people. Yes indeed, if I ever break up with the love of my life, this guy will be the first in line.

> looking for a new play mate and needs to be total sud for i am a respectful dom.
> let me know if your interested????

What is a sud? Is that like one soap bubble?

> yes i have seen some of your exiting videos your boyfrend is lucky. tel mee where can i get nice pictures of you or nice pictures stiles discpliniriane d wife club.tank you it is very hard to find a spanking partner .

Hard to find a spanking partner? Gee, I wonder why.

> interested well i see your in a relationship i am aswell but i would love to be able to spank you ..ur.. pretty sexy an beautiful ....ur husbang is a lucky man but i wisj i was that lucky!

Thank you, but I don't have a husbang. I'm not marrieg.

> hello sexy how r u? i want to chat with u on msn sexy xxxxxx ilike u so much sweety u look so nice can u send me your msn or yahoo to chat now xxxx many kissessssssssss

Sweetheart, I'm broadcasting your idiocy to all of blogdom. I'm really not that nice.

> Each plant has a message in it, listen to its vibration if all my thoughts were a flower, the world will be a huge garden for you and if you want to masturbate with me, it will make me a great pleasure to admire this beautiful body that you with love

Say what? Whatever plants he's ingesting, I want some.

> hey babycake what's up ? whould u like to see
> my sexy monster of mine=)LOL u should try=)
> just give ur messenger hun im wating 4 ur
> message... kisses muck..=)

Muck is right.

> i would spank you if i could but im all the way in
> the united states.... lol....

And where am I, Siberia?

> hi there male 34 from calif to that spanks for
> discplien woudl teach u lesson to be good grl im
> single write to me

According to this gentleman's SpankFinder profile,
he's 34, lives with his parents, and his favorite "Hot
Spot" is Applebee's. And he's single?? Say it ain't so.

On Alt.com, this man disregarded everything I
said about seeking spanking, not sex, and wrote me a
long discourse on his sexual prowess. Here's a
portion:

> I have studied tartaric Buddhism and the Kuma
> Sutra. I'm into mind and verbal errotic foreplay.
> I enjoy having "more" than one orgsim within
> one session and love to go for a long, long time.

Orgsim?? The Kuma Sutra? And what in the world is
"tartaric Buddhism"? Does he worship tartar sauce?
Ew.

> have u ever sent someone ur pabties yet?

My what? Sorry, I'm not familiar with pabties, so I'm quite certain I've never sent them.

Then, a couple of days later, same guy:

hi love ur pics , i was wondering how u would feel about sending me a pair of ur panties?

Oh, panties! Why didn't you say so? In that case…no.

cum to me in vegas using my decades of experience make your kitty purr in exotuc sex grampa master xxx

I've got news for you, grampa. The only thing that gets me to Vegas is the Shadow Lane parties. My kitty can purr just fine right here at home, thank you very much.

But wait, there's more. This guy was on Alt.com—check out his profile blurb:

Iam a 72 year ould white male that likes esotic sex. IM LOOKING FOR A TOTALLY uninhibited woman for kinky sex. I AM VERY ORAL ACTIVE.

And here I thought it was just the Text Generation who couldn't spell. Pray tell, what is *esotic*? Did he mean exotic, erotic, or esoteric? And is it just me, or does Oral Active sound like a good name for a new mouthwash?

I honestly don't know whether to laugh or cry at the next one:

(first of all you have a nice ass--saw your pics.) and I have to admit.. saw your profile pic and I thought maybe you were a former man..OK that being said Iam intriqued watching and lookin at people... wonder what happens to you after a spanking.(ha big hands and feet). and would like it if you could use um. (has this fantasy of being blindolded).question.are you interested?

Whoa. Back up. I'm having a little trouble getting past that first comment. No, not the one about my nice ass; the one about my looking like a former man. Say what?

My mind reels with responses to that, and most of them are quite obscene. So I'll put it to you folks instead. Many of you have met me in person. Others have seen several pictures of me, have seen me on video. Tell me...Do I look like I have a FUCKING Y CHROMOSOME to you?

Allow me to set the record straight. I have ovaries. I have all the requisite girl gear, and I was born with it, thank you.

Moving on. As for the rest of this disjointed mess, is it possible to decipher it without the aid of recreational substances? I doubt it, but I'll attempt to parse it anyway.

What happens to me after a spanking? Only my spanker gets to know.

Ha big hands and feet? WTF? Is he saying I have big hands and feet? Are we back to the former man thing again?

"Would like it if you could use um..." Um, what? Speak up, Junior. Use your words.

"Has this fantasy of being blindolded" [sic]—My turn to go "um." What does that have to do with anything?

"question.are you interested?" In what? Never mind. Don't answer that. If it has anything to do with you, the answer is no.

And finally, if you want to people-watch, I suggest you go to Walmart. Really, I'm not all that "intriqueing."

Sheeesh. Every time I think I've heard it all, someone adds to the Encyclopedia Stupidica.

if yoou would like someone to put his handsome head under that skirt and please let it be me

Yup, that's the first thing I think when I see an attractive man: "Put that head up my skirt!" Oh, and I saw your picture. Apparently you have access to a stunt handsome head.

I am a 6'1" 190lbs professional who is very outgoing, respectful and well endowed if thats's important (8 inches and 5.7 round).

First off, no, it's not important, unless you're planning on spanking me with your endowment. And second, 5.7?? The exactness of that measurement cracks me up. Not 5 1/2, not 5 3/4, but 5.7. Really? How do you get a precise measurement when you're in that state, anyway? Aren't your hands shaking just a little?

Here's something else I love—guys I don't know from Adam who send long, horribly written, graphic sex/spanking stories to me. I received one of those

143

this week; no introduction, nothing but the story. Some drivel about a woman going to a movie theater by herself and having a sexual encounter with a mysterious stranger who sits next to her. It went on and on and it was rather pornographic, so I'll spare you the bulk of it. Here are just a few snippets:

> The pair of hands working in unison and semetrically, worked their way accross her color bone and fingers began to enter the top of her v-neck sweater.

Color bone??

> The mouth was back to her ear again sucked and lick for such a quick secound that it almost didn't seem real if it hadn't been for the cool sensation on her ear left by the wettnes of the toungue.

No wettnes here, pal.

> there was a moment of slowing down and guaging if it would reall fit or not, she was out of her mind by now, and taking deep breathes to relax her self.

By this point, I was taking deep *breathes* to keep my self from hurling my breakfast. Don't quit your day job, dear. Hemingway, you ain't.

> My photo current but I may or may not have a goat tee that comes and goes.

Does anyone else get an image in their head of a goat in a T-shirt running in and out of this guy's living room?

> If you have the time to figure this out at sometime we can chat and then we can get to know ea. other and you can get some male descreet companionship and wouldn't dot be wonderful if we could com(e) together sometime.

If I have the time to figure this out? No one has *that* much time, honey.

> i want to do a video with u,spanking and maybe also with my fucking machine..

Oh, the humanity. They have machines for everything now.

> i luv to eat them sexy panty off u right now sweety i want u

I don't know quite how to break this to you, sweety, but I'm not wearing edible underwear. You try to eat them off me and you'll learn the meaning of cotton-mouth.

> Very pretty Girl !
> And a nice ass.... I like it..I like it..I like it.....YES I LIKE IT!

Why do I feel like Sally Field? ("You LIKE my ass! You really, really like it!")

I am Xxxxx and quite enjoyed your strawberry'd
ass which is what sparked my imagination to
bend you over my knee and hear what a dirty
little girl you have been and hear some of those
thoughts 1st hand as I bring my pig paw down
on your bareness...

Frankly, he lost me at strawberry'd ass. And I am
not a dirty little girl, thank you. I have absolutely no
desire to be spanked by a pig paw.

well how are u doing tonight? I hope u are well.
I know your not near me but your not that far
away:) So I love too chat with u and get to
know u better and see if we hit it off I love too
give u good spanking:)...So I hope too hear from
u and look forward too chatting with u and
getting too know u a better. want too know or
see anything else ask away

You misspelled "to" six times. I think I've seen
enough.

Your either the hugest prick tease in the world
or the most understanding, loving person Ive
ever met ? I wish so very much I could meet
you in person till it hurts !!

Wha...? Was I just complimented or dissed? How
did he arrive at those two extreme polarities? What
constitutes prick-teasing, anyway? Sexy pictures? So,
are all women in the spanko scene/industry prick-
teases? And regarding my being the most
understanding and loving person...how did I go

from Tanya Temptress to Mother Teresa in one sentence?

> Im one who knows how to please...and please again until wettness over comes you .

Would that wettness be from my tears of laughter?

> I am new to this, hope thqt is not an issuhe. I would love to explore and spanking would be one of them, if you are into teaching I would love to lern.

I don't teach. And if you can't even spell *learn*, I doubt you could do it.

> WHAT ! What do I say to youl ? I will say, tell me what you want me to do and I will as long as you say to ! I'd swallow all yours.

All my what? Never mind; don't answer that. What do you say to me? How about goodbye?

Recently, I received this:

> I am Xxxx from IL. you are hot.

Harmless, I thought. So I wrote back, "Thank you."
Next day, I got seven—count them, seven—messages from this guy:

> What are you up to?
> I am home all day by myself

U wanna talk today!

Can you send more pics?.Wanna see me?

talk to me! What do you want to show
what do you want 2 see

do you wanna talk online?

taking a sick day
make sure we can keep in touch

Hi got a camera
What do you want to see?

Good lord. I want to see you go away. Please. Enjoy your sick day and go cruise porn.

There are two creatures fighting in a woman: a cat who wants to walk by herself and a dog who needs a master.

Is that so? Well, the cat in me wants to claw that smug look off your face, and the dog in me wants to poop on your shoes. How would that work for you?

having any luck getting your butt beat? ever feel the rubber strap on your ass? it well leave a welp

No, it won't. It will leave a welt or a weal, dumbass.

> Hello ... I am just your friendly neighboorhood pervert who loves spanking female asses and fucking them ... LOL

Note his spelling of "neighborhood." There is truth in typos.

> Like your pix's and your bottom.......
> Would love to spank..kiss and lick it..

You know, "pix" is short for pictures. Therefore, adding apostrophe + s to pix is redundant and makes you look stupid. Just thought you might like to know.

> yhat is a sweet lil' ass. :) i'd enjoy making it red... and watching you drip from the sting.

It's not the sting that makes me drip; it's the man administering it. And in your case, I'd be the Sahara desert.

> You can be my slut anytime, sweetmeat.

Wow, I can? Really? Cool! And you can go blow yourself anytime, mincemeat.

> i cant beleave how hot and sexy you are in your photo i love it so much.nothing is as nice as you nothing.you are like so hot.the pleasure in you is so feels beautyful .....you seem like such a cool lady ,i know im maybe not your typ but i had to say this anyways either way.

Honey, you're definitely not my typ.

> I think you have a great smile and a perfect - - -
> thought I was going to say "ass" didn't you,
> great bottom. Would love to be able to caress
> and feel both, before spanking the ladder.

Ouch! Better sand that ladder first or you'll get splinters.

> hi erica not only do I have a spanking fetish but
> also woman wear slips very hard to find both
> together. Maybe naughty girl.wearing skirt/slip
> over a woman's knee also wearing a dress and
> slip thanks.

Does anyone wear slips anymore? I don't own any. Too bad, because this guy sounds like quite the prize.

> I live in Honolulu. I have a very good job, you
> must be willing to move in with me in Hawaii. I
> am 44 years old 5,10 175lbs, work out three
> times a week at 24 hour fitness. Like your
> profile. Single and looking for a wife .you sound
> perfect. if you are willing to relocate reply back
> at we can get to know each oter better.

Oooh, a marriage proposal! And I'm perfect for him—oh, except for that pesky boyfriend of mine. Oh, and the fact that I have no intention of relocating anywhere (I don't see him offering up the money for me to do that, either). Oh, and I have no desire to ever marry. But other than that, it's a match made in heaven!

> My name is Xxx and I am 25 years old! I was wondering if maybe you wanted to do some online sessions! I think you are really quite cute and would love to punish you! Maybe we could work it out to do a real sessions!
> Thanks for the time, Xxx!

Someone needs to disable this guy's exclamation point key. Can you imagine doing an online session with him? "Bad girl! Hold still! Smack! Smack! You need to be punished! I'm going to punish you! I'm taking you over my knee right now!!!!"

> I would enjoy indulging in your ass, luv.

Why do I get the feeling that my butt is a pint of Ben & Jerry's?

The next gentleman seems to be a photographer who is critiquing one of my pictures. Hard to tell with all the illiteracy.

> working on the photo thing would LOVE to do a lot better than I saw in your pics. and warm your ass up a little more. was disapointed you were not tied to te chair. but really enjoyed the fact you had a garte belt and stocking on

Perhaps you should work on the writing thing instead.

your bottom needs more redesspurple to it
hummmmm..nice thights very nice!!!

Pray tell, what color is redesspurple? I don't recall
that one from my Crayola 64-Pack.

im the one. I want u... I love 2 show my women
I care with pain.. Let me show u

Your profile picture already showed me your dick. I
don't need to see anymore.

Another thing that I have clearly stated, many times,
is that I'm not into the Daddy/daughter dynamic.
Nothing wrong with it; just not my thing. And yet...

daddy likes what he sees. u r a butt beaiufull
bottom i love u over my knee n bare r bottom n
give u the spanking - croping u need need n
have a taste for i am know for my o t k style call
if u like to go for a trip over my knee that
botton is in real need for attion i travl for work
wwe com phone xxx xxx xxxx w-male xxx xxx
xxxx if u r real call hope to see u soon

Let's review. 1) You're not my Daddy. I'm no
genius, but there's no way I could be the spawn of
someone so stupid. 2) No, I don't want to go for a
trip over your knee. We've already discussed how
much I hate to travel. 3) I doubt you are know [sic]
for your OTK style. More likely you are know [sic]
for writing like a first-grader.
 Two more:

> you seem hot..if you are into Anal Sex or want too try, Daddy would be willing to teach or play with you?

1. I'm old enough to be your mother, you twit. I'm not calling you Daddy. 2. If suddenly pigs started flying and I decided I wanted too [sic] try Anal Sex, it wouldn't be with you.

> You need a Hot Daddy. I acn take care of you.

No, you acn't.

> Hi..there.I'm bored & just checkin things out.I cant take my eyes off your profile pics.I wana say,"u got a very gorgeous spankable firm Bottom.I'm very turned-on by your already stinged redden cheeks.

Stinged? Did he mean singed? Stung?
I'm sorry you're bored. Try reading a book. There are some really cute pop-up ones available on Amazon.

> all i want to do is give u a good spnking every time i come to town i visit my kids there in fresno and i pass thru ur town once a month so get back too me and maybe u will be dropping ur drawers for me sometime soon

Dropping my drawers?
My town is nowhere near Fresno, But sure, come on over. I'll drop a fully loaded dresser drawer on your foot.

> Hey sexy gorgeous I will u a full body with candle lights and shared some wine with you and giving u a nice kiss!! How are u?

At the moment, perplexed. You will me a full body with candle lights? I'm sorry you died, but really, couldn't you just give it to charity? There are so many unfortunate half-full bodies out there.

> When you get your bare ass spank does the man stop now an then to rub an massage your bare ass to keep it from tighten up an keep it loose so you could feel every smack sure hope so.

Please tell me I just imagined this one. It's too depressing to think people actually write this badly. Trust me, I feel every smack, tight ass or loose ass.

> I'am a very nice looking, 5'10", 175 lb man with a great physique, seeking a submissive female that wants adventure in the realm of submission. Looking for that girl that needs to be trained in the ways of submission...... or are you the woman that knows her roll. The adventure waits for that special girl/women.....are you the one? That special female that wants enjoy the adventure of submissiveness while receiving the attention deserved

Redundant, much? Hmmm. Do I know my roll? Perhaps it's crescent, or could it be Kaiser? Oh, wait!

154

Parker House! Parker House rolls kinda look like little bottoms, don't they?

> I am interested in gentle dildo training.

I should think you are. Because one should never train one's dildo harshly.

> hello do you enjoy face sitting if so would you like to turn my face into your set and sit on it as long as you like or wear my face like its your panties

Ye gods. You attached your picture; I've seen your face. I don't want to sit on it, wear it, or ever see it again.

> Instinctively i liked your profile. You seem like a soft and mature woman at it's most greedy for everything that is good and yummy.

I'm not an it, I am a she. Yes, I'm greedy for yummy good writing. At the moment, I'm starving.

Here's my first CHoS entry received via tweet!

> I am taking my good stinging straps from my freezer and I wil meat u on my lap in 6.9 minites

How do you measure 6.9 minutes?? I suppose it could be done with a sophisticated chronometer, but I doubt this dumbass would know how to read one.

This guy on Alt wrote to me. His profile bore zero resemblance to mine, and he was older than what I specifically requested, so I didn't reply. A week later, I got this:

> Why won't you let me spank you??? We can meet for a coffee or lunch and see how it goes and move on from there. You pic the place in your are that you feel comfortible with.

I still didn't reply, but really wanted to write the following:

"Why? Well, let's see:
1. You're several years older than my crystal-clear stated age range, and you look 10 years older than your age;
2. You can't type three sentences without making three errors; and
3. Your profile states that you're especially interested in women who wish to learn how to lactate. Wrong anatomical region, pal. I don't have milk glands in my butt. Move on."

> When we're you last punished? Don't you feel that twinge right down to your clit Erica ?

None of you're—I mean, *your* business.

> Hi Darling
> you are totally fuckable
> I am in LA a lot

Well, good for you, Snookums. Feel free to pass by my apartment when you're in town. And then keep going.

> Hi my dear,
>
> Love your beautiful body. I'm a lusty single guy with an absurdly strong libido & a desire to explore our wildest fantasy's. My work making your body quiver & reach your sexual peak comes from years of experience.. Wanna make it happen?

Thank you so much for the naked photo. I was particularly impressed with how your big quivering belly hangs over your absurdly small dick.

> Love the pixtures and if I could read I would know what to wright about.....
> Please pick me!
> It would make the world we live in all-right and all that is good would reappear.
> Please understand I have not a clue what to say here....
> And I like to LOL around....hence the rambling.
> Call me
> [name and phone number deleted]
> Ps I am much better on. The phone and even betted live and in person. LoL

(groan) Well, at least he's spot on about being clueless. Ah, if only things were that simple, if picking him would make the entire universe all-right...er, all wright...I mean...Oh, forget it.

I like to think that My training of submissives/slaves is very good.

And I like to think I'm 25. We all have our fantasies.

hi hunn you look hot and kinky if u like torture and extremely sadistic things i would like to talk?

Well, hunn, just reading this was torture enough, thanks much.

Ki..

I am a ass and tit man, love spanking and suking. But.. like you have someone for sex, so I just enjoy the BDSM part of this culture.

So if ya would like to try my style, lets talk..

Who the hell is Ki? I think I'll pass on trying your style, hon. It suks.

Hi do you like Young Adult Guy's like mysself i am 22Yro and I have to be Honest i do have a GF aka Wifey who I realy Love but I do Like you and I have never had a Jewish oldrer women before who looks like she is always's in her 20's seriously so can I ask you how big is your breasts and circles around your nipples and are they light brown or dark brown or tan and do you have a webcam so get back to me asap.

Oy. Honest, huh? Do you tell your GF/Wifey that you're writing crap like this to *oldrer* women?

This one has the dubious distinction of being last. Sometimes, I'd get these missives and laugh out loud with delight, because they were such perfect CHoS entries. The following was most definitely in that category.

> 254 miles is only a hot rainbow to the pot of hot steaming love gold. So let's cash it in for pleasure beautiful goddesses of my passion. That I hold deep in side my soul that only a lady of desire would understand..........let's email this and follow the rainbow ....my love.

There's something hot and steaming here, but it's not gold. You're 254 miles from me? Good. Stay there. Please.

After pages and pages of this nonsense, I feel the need to end on a positive note. Because, despite the plethora of unsavory messages I've collected, they don't compare to the many more kind, sweet, complimentary, funny, and touching notes people have taken the time to write to me.

Turn the page and see just how lovely some folks can be.

SHINY DIAMONDS

Many years ago, I heard someone say this at a 12-step meeting: "Be grateful for the assholes in your life. They help you appreciate the good folks." I suppose that's one way of making lemonade out of lemons! I do indeed appreciate these good folks, more than anyone can imagine, even without the dubious input of the jackasses.

Even though I've gotten a lot of the bad stuff from Alt.com, I've also met three fabulous tops there (including my current one). When I was seeing my former top, ST, a couple of years ago, people would ask, "Where did you find this guy?" and be shocked when I said Alt. I liked to say that I dug through the slimy slagheap and came up with a shiny diamond.

I'm going to close this book with a couple of gems from people who got it right; whose words brought a smile to my face and lifted my spirits. People who know how to reach out and express a kind thought, a word of appreciation or support, a sincere compliment. For everyone who has taken the time to do this, I thank you.

A while back on FetLife, a gentleman I didn't know went through my photos and posted a "Love" on several dozen of them. Coming on and seeing that was a pleasant treat, so I dropped him a note, saying, "Thank you for all the love!" He wrote back:

> Thank you for sharing your adventures. You are very beautiful and I like how much the camera loves you, your expressive face and eyes and the way you carry yourself. You have model

good looks and a great ability to look through the camera. My sincere compliments.

Wow. From a complete stranger, too. Isn't that delightful?

This next man is not a stranger, but he started out as one who reached out to me, asking questions about the scene, as he was about to be brave and take his first leap into it. Long story short, we corresponded a bit, he started coming to parties and we met, and now he is a treasured friend, a lovely man who has brought much joy to our scene in a short time. A couple of months ago, I had posted a blog about friendships; I was feeling sad, realizing that the trade-off for being a loner and commanding a lot of space and solitude is to not have many close friends in my life. This gentleman wrote a long email to me, expressing such loving and kind thoughts about me, I bawled. Most of it is personal and I will keep it private and close to my heart, but I will share this snippet:

Thank you for strength.
Thank you for guidance.
Thank you for friendship.
Thank you for amazing play. (AMAZING)
Thank you for laughs.
Thank you for hugs.
Thank you for being the woman who has done so much to make the spanking community all that it is today.
I'm honored to be in your circle and I, my dear, do. love. you.

There go the waterworks again. Thank *you*, dear.

When my autobiography *Late Bloomer* came out, I got a lot of beautiful messages from people who had read and enjoyed it. Most touching of all were the young women who said my words resonated with them and gave them courage to follow their own path. One such woman wrote a detailed, emotionally open email, and it ended with this:

> I love your spirit, Erica. You are strong and feisty and complex and kind and very giving (as was evidenced by your even having written this book) and I feel that you are very much a kindred spirit to me, and very much an inspiration. So...a heartfelt thank you. I wish I could describe how much having read your book meant to me.

I think you just did, sweetheart. Thank you.

And finally—last year, I lost a beloved play partner of nearly two years. I called him ST on my blogs and we had many wonderful adventures. He met a new girlfriend, and unfortunately, she didn't care for his relationship with me. So I had to say goodbye.

Around the same time as I was losing ST, I heard from another man on Alt.com. I was impressed with him from the start. First, he'd read my entire profile and acknowledged the salient points. Second, he'd attached two pictures, both of his face, thank you (and he was cute as hell). And third, he knew the difference between "it's" and its." (Yes, this impresses me.) So I wrote back, and we eventually took it off Alt and onto email. I told him of my current situation, of how I was in a transition period,

162

mourning the loss of a top to whom I'd been very close. How I wanted to play, but wasn't sure if I was emotionally ready to start all over again with someone new. He was very understanding, didn't push anything, and showed nothing but respect for my feelings, assuring me that he would not try to replace ST and he would accommodate my timetable.

Here's a portion of an email he sent to me, after I blogged about my last session with ST:

> I was both sad and excited when reading your latest blog about your final session with [ST] (or at least for a while). I could feel your sadness and how much you will miss him. As well, I was thinking about that "when one door closes, another opens" phrase. Maybe you and I have met at this time for a reason. Fate? Coincidence? I don't know. But what I do know is that I'd love to be chosen for at least an opportunity to show my worthiness to you. Are you free next Monday?...oh, yes, you are!
>
> I'd love to talk with you and be a part of your "emotional processing" if you are up for talking about it with me. In a way I can see that process as being a possible bridge...on one side you and [ST]...on the other, me waiting for you with open arms, and with a nice riding crop in hand.

How could I resist someone who wrote like this? I didn't. This kind stranger became my friend and my top, and he still is.

And of course, the man who wrote me a poem after our first meeting and has written many more since, is still my love, 17 years later. I am a very lucky woman.

So I have to deal with some asshats now and then. Put into perspective, it's not so bad. Especially since I can have some fun with it. Thanks for playing along, and for reading my blog all these years.

If you'd like to say hello, or if you'd ever like to share your own examples of horrible missives you've received, please do! My blog's email address is erica.scott.blog@gmail.com. Who knows, maybe if I get enough material, someday I could compile a CHoS, Book II.

(How some of my readers imagine me at the computer, I suppose!)

Made in the USA
Lexington, KY
05 November 2013